TOTAL BUSINESS DESIGN

TOTAL BUSINESS DESIGN

NEIL FARMER and BOB LANKESTER

JOHN WILEY & SONS

Chichester · New York · Brisbane · Toronto · Singapore

Other Wiley Editorial Offices

John Wiley & Sons, Inc., 605 Third Avenue,
New York, NY 10158-0012, USA

Jacaranda Wiley Ltd, 33 Park Road, Milton,
Queensland 4064, Australia

John Wiley & Sons (Canada) Ltd, 22 Worcester Road,
Rexdale, Ontario M9W 1L1, Canada

John Wiley & Sons (Asia) Pte Ltd, 2 Clementi Loop #02-01,
Jin Xing Distripark, Singapore 0512

British Library Cataloguing in Publication Data

A catalogue record for this book is available from the British Library

ISBN 0–471–96479–4

Produced from camera-ready copy supplied by the authors
Printed and bound in Great Britain by Biddles Ltd, Guildford and King's Lynn

Contents

DS8
8
F368
996

Acknowledgements

This book was written by Neil Farmer to encapsulate almost three years of intensive work with Bob Lankester, researching and developing a much-needed, complete and coherent approach to successful business transformation.

It is dedicated to all those senior executives, change agents and management consultants who not only had the courage to admit to levels of failure, but also were prepared to discuss them.

The authors' gratitude is extended to the client organisations who allowed them to viability test the TBD concepts during live projects. Also, to friends and associates in the consulting community who lent their experiences, advice and encouragement – particularly, Mark Rogers, Peter Feltham and John Slocombe.

Worthy of special mention are:

- George Cox, a past Member of Council of the Institute of Management Consultants and current Managing Director of Information Services Group Europe, Unisys, for editing the book during his Christmas break, so that "the strong messages in the book are not obscured by the words".

- David Redwood, Chairman of the Largotim Group, for his support and advice.

- Linda Richards, for using her graphics and desktop publishing skills – often under intense pressure – to produce this book.

- Our families, for allowing themselves to be bored rigid without complaint (well almost!) during the last three years.

Preface – The birth of an insight

Like most management consultants and business change researchers over the last decade and more, Neil Farmer and Bob Lankester
were frustrated.

Neil ran one of Europe's largest change research organisations and,
in the 1980s and early 1990s, witnessed the birth of a steady stream
of new ideas that promised to revitalise western businesses. Yet as
each new research study delved beneath the initial hype and the
'good news' stories in the business press, a steady pattern of high
levels of failure in major business change programmes emerged.

During the same period, Bob worked with some of the world's most
senior executives in trying to gain real business benefits from these
'transformation' ideas. While he saw some significant gains in
business practice and even profitability in many of his clients, he
nevertheless was not immune from the growing patterns of business transformation failure. Somehow, even in the most successful
assignments where clients waxed lyrical about what had been
achieved, he had a strong feeling that opportunities were being
missed and that much more needed to be done. All too often the
'second and third prizes' were achieved, while a seemingly diverse
mixture of internal politics, technological complexity, changing
business environments, and human inertia led to the really impressive prizes being delayed into the indeterminate future.

In 1992, both the authors began work on a single insight that seemed
to be consistent with the high failure rates being reported in major
business change. The clues that led to this insight were many and
varied. Business strategies based on ideas such as 'Critical Success
Factors' and 'Value Chain Analysis' reported high failure rates;
quality improvement and cultural change programmes were widely
seen as "running out of steam"; Business Process Reengineering
was being heavily hyped even as the initial failures were being
whispered to researchers during quiet, off the record, lunches.
Other 'transformation' ideas were also suffering seemingly similar
patterns of failure.

At a memorable brainstorm event in a lovely county mansion hotel in southern England in 1992, one participant dared to put the growing frustration into a simple phrase:

"It seems that every business transformation idea ever invented has a failure rate of 70% or 80% or more .... what on earth is going on?"

Indirectly, and some months later, this outburst led to the (quite obvious) insight that:

"The likelihood of success or failure in any major business transformation initiative is largely independent of the business design ideas being used."

During a four-year period from 1992 to late 1995, we researched the validity (or otherwise) of this radical insight. This exercise proved to be one of the most difficult pieces of research that we have ever undertaken. We were researching very high levels of real failure in major areas of change in (mainly) quite large organisations, where personal careers were at stake ...... and where modest success could be used to obscure failure to achieve much larger benefits.

We quickly learnt that traditional (on the record) interviews with senior executives often produced biased and optimistic interpretations of what was really happening. So we based most of our initial research on off-the-record discussions with those directly responsible for implementing change programmes. Bland statements and assumptions were rigorously challenged, adverse change experiences in other businesses were discussed, realistic balances were made between what had really been achieved and what might yet be possible, and gradually a picture approximating to the truth usually emerged ..... to the satisfaction of some very cynical researchers and change consultants. Some of the most incisive and detailed information was gleaned from extremely frustrated individuals speaking frankly about their thwarted ambitions over lunch tables and in bars.

Having gleaned the 'bad news' from those who had tried hard and failed in the 'business transformation game', we then drew on their lessons from failure to ask very specific questions of senior executives involved in current major change initiatives. By adopting an off-the-record position, and by relating to specific problems experienced in other businesses, we were then able to confirm almost all of the previously identified hurdles to success in major change exercises.

At the time of writing, we have carried out detailed, face-to-face, discussions with over 100 individuals in 46 different businesses, and have received relevant information at a less-detailed level (through questionnaires, telephone discussions, consultant discussions and secondary literature searches) on the change initiatives at a further 180 businesses.

Almost four years after the memorable 1992 brainstorm, and as we finish writing this book, we know that the original insight has some constraints .... but that it will nevertheless profoundly alter the way that business change is viewed in future. Radical one-off changes, continuous improvement, and every practical learning organisation will all (sooner or later) be strongly influenced by the implications of this simple insight.

This book explains why.

~ 1 ~
The 80%+ failure rule

Business transformation is in a mess. Cultural change programmes, quality initiatives and business process reengineering are all becoming dirty words. Even some of the much-vaunted early examples of dramatic business success are becoming tainted.

The following quotes illustrate the current state of disillusion:

- A T Kearney: "80% of quality programmes in the UK fail"

- Michael Hammer: "about 70% of business process reengineering projects fail"

- Tom Peters: "90% of cultural change programmes fail"

- Tom Davenport: "the hype about reengineering will die down. I just hope the whole thing doesn't go with it."

Our own research into more than 200 businesses in Europe and North America that have attempted business transformations of various kinds between 1990 and 1995 makes even sadder reading:

- Less than 5% of business transformation exercises lead to real 'transformation' across the business.

- Less than 20% of business transformation exercises achieve notable piecemeal successes.

- More than 80% of business transformation exercises achieve very little, or nothing at all.

Those who view these findings with an optimistic eye might conclude that we are at an early stage of business transformation experience, moving cautiously, and that the number of real successes with grow steadily in future years. And to a *limited* degree they are probably right.

The real problem, however, is that business transformation has become a fashion industry in recent years. Ideas that don't gain a good reputation reasonably rapidly are likely to be overlooked in favour of the latest whizz approach. Consultants make much money each time, businesses are disrupted without gaining significant advantages, and the sorry statistics of failure are repeated.

The problem will persist for all those who don't change the rules of the game.

~ 2 ~
Objective

The premise behind this book is extremely simple and very fundamental. It is that executives and other business 'influencers' should be trained as professional business 'designers' and change managers, working in 'learning' organisations.

We argue that a new, much more professional, cadre of business people will arise from this process. These people will be confident enough to recognise that the primary role of new managers is to get the 'design' of the business right, and that all major business success and failure flows primarily from this design.

No longer will uncertain executives hide behind management consultants. Indeed, the management consultancy industry will undergo major change, as their clients acquire business design skills and create a very different corporate world.

The most immediate objective of our book is to help businesses reverse the current 80%+ failure rate of business transformation. The underlying objective is to accelerate the inevitable trend towards professional 'Total Business Design'.

The layout of the book encourages browsing, although it may be read from cover to cover in less than three hours.

Our target readers are senior business executives who do not have the time to read worthy tomes describing new business approaches. For those who are seeking to identify the real 'signals' of business change amongst the background chatter, read on ......

~ 3 ~
Business transformation: the need

Any senior executive who does not believe that there is a need to transform the way the business 'machine' operates as we approach the end of the twentieth century need read no further. This book is not for you.

For those of you who are still reading, it will be clear that something very special is required to slow or reverse the trend towards dominance by new and emerging economies such as Japan, the Pacific basin, China, and even (eventually) Eastern Europe and South America.

Above all, we need to recognise that the way the business machine has operated in the past is just no longer appropriate for the future. We also need to recognise that many of the so-called solutions to these problems are superficial and over-hyped.

As you browse through this book, please bear in mind the following requirements for business success at the end of the millennium:

- Business products must continually be adapted to achieve or sustain competitive advantage. While some of these changes will be due to individual inspiration, most progress will be made by focusing inspiration through a professional team approach to optimise real business opportunities.

- The ills induced by a system of management by 'command and control' within a rigid hierarchy need to be addressed in a balanced and effective way. The twin aims of an intelligent and effective workforce combined with low costs can only be achieved by consigning most, *but not all*, hierarchical structures to the dustbin of history.

- If we are to achieve this elusive combination of business intelligence and business efficiency, we need to recruit, motivate and work with the right people. This will not happen by accident. It is very unlikely indeed that your existing people mix is really your 'biggest corporate asset'.

These primary requirements can only be achieved by getting the underlying business design right. We need to reject fashion as the way forward and concentrate on using the best design tools for this very difficult job. The only approach at our disposal that will survive the multiple changes, new ideas, fads and fashions as we enter the twenty-first century is ....Total Business Design.

What is Total Business Design?

Total Business Design is a flexible, practical framework for a true learning organisation. It describes an approach to modelling and successfully implementing a wide range of business design combinations, based on lessons learnt from the widespread failures of business transformation in the past.

The three main components of the Total Business Design framework represent solutions to the confusion that currently abounds in business transformation. These components are:

- A selection process that enables you to choose the most appropriate business design ideas for your business (this year), and not rely on the latest management change fashions.

- An original change management approach that maximises the chances of successful major business change being achieved.

- A blueprint for a successful learning organisation, based on both of the above, that contains mechanisms for both radical change and ongoing continuous improvement.

Where existing design ideas have been shown to work, we have adopted these. Where totally new approaches have been needed, we have developed and incorporated them into our framework.

Perhaps the best analogy to illustrate the nature of Total Business Design is to consider a highly competent economics commentator, such as Peter Jay, the BBC's current Economics Editor. When government policies change or when a new set of economic indicators are published, Peter's analysis is highly clinical and clearly based on his underlying mental model of how an economy works. New approaches can be incorporated into his model and the resulting analysis modified accordingly. In contrast, lesser analysts offer only superficial, piecemeal comments.

Similarly, the scope of our framework covers business designs ranging in character from core business concepts, through once fashionable process reengineering and TQM, to motivational designs and even the use of manufacturing approaches in service/administrative environments. New design ideas can be added to the model at will.

Our framework also includes very strong elements of original change management/transition techniques to measure and then maximise the chances of successful major change implementation.

Our learning organisation framework helps to ensure that the business design and change management lessons learnt from successful change then become incorporated into practical mechanisms for future change.

During the remainder of this book, we consider the current confused state of business transformation before examining each ingredient of the current Total Business Design model.

We look at the high failure rate of business transformation exercises, the main reasons for failure, ideas that break the mould, implementing major change effectively, implementing a practical learning organisation, and using (or not using) consultants. You and your colleagues can accept, reject or modify these ingredients to create your own highly specific design for *your* business.

Total Business Design represents a breakthrough in business transformation because of the power of its underlying model. Once the model becomes second nature, no piecemeal new idea (promoted by the latest management guru) will ever seem the same again.

~ 5 ~
Main reasons for failure

The very depressing statistics for success in business transformation prompted us to ask the fundamental question:

"Why is business transformation success so elusive?"

To assess the nature of the problem, we first took an introspective look at the consultancy industry, aiming to identify factors that may have contributed to this outrageous level of failure. We questioned whether the array of techniques used by the major consultancies, such as business process reengineering, total quality management or core business concepts could really facilitate major change. Many have been 'packaged' by the big consultancy firms and have lost a cutting business edge after being trawled round from company to company. Despite this, however, there is much evidence to suggest, that in the right circumstances, many of these approaches can be applied effectively. Only a minority of major change approaches are seriously flawed in themselves, although many are oversold.

Most large businesses have also suffered from some consultancy firms deliberately extending the length of projects, in an exercise to maximise fees. Despite widespread superficial evidence of this practice, however, we concluded that the problem is more fundamental than greedy consultants.

We then focused our research on businesses attemptingmajor transformation and identified four major hurdles to effective change in medium and large-sized organisations. We believe that overcoming these hurdles will radically improve the chances of success in major transformation exercises.

The four are lack of commitment, piecemeal fashion-driven approaches, ineffective change training and lethargic IT systems.

Lack of commitment

Lack of commitment is the chief reason behind failed business transformation exercises: not that commitment is missing at the top, it simply fails to permeate the lower, and equally essential, levels.

What is actually required for success is commitment from a number of what we call *key influencers*. It is often difficult to identify these influencers because they do not reside at obvious levels of management. Key influencers can be located in *several levels* of the organisation, although the majority will typically reside near the top. When senior executives attempt to identify key influencers at lower levels, they usually get at least one-third of the people wrong.

These key influencers are the catalysts for change, and their support is critical to the success of all major change initiatives affecting the business machine.

This is one of the principal findings of our research and is the foundation for our unique approach to change management. Without the genuine commitment of enough key influencers, only a partial level of organisational commitment exists, and only limited, very high-level structural and employee numbers changes are likely to be achieved.

In essence therefore, we believe that the major cause of the poor track record of business transformation is a lack of commitment at board *and* key influencer levels.

Any approach to change management that promises to reverse the 80%+ failure rule must seriously grasp the 'commitment' nettle .... and the solutions must be practical, not just wishful, theoretical or laced with motherhood statements.

What senior executives can achieve by themselves and what they can't

Design tools	Implemented by executives	Implemented by executives with help from other 'influencers'
Core business changes	√	
Outsourcing	√	
People numbers changes	√	
Business process redesign		√
Empowerment		√
Multiskilling		√
Continuous improvement		√
Strategic alliances	√	
'Smallness' of business units	√	

Note: Senior executives can make effective high-level, structural and employee size changes without the active support of other key influencers. But they need an overall positive balance of opinion amongst other key influencers if they are to achieve effective, significant changes in the way the business 'machine' works.

Piecemeal, fashion-driven approaches

An arbitrary set of business design techniques have been combined into fashionable mixes that address business change in piecemeal ways. This inevitably leads to a blinkered implementation and limits the scope for business optimisation.

In practice, what this really means is that even if you are good enough (or lucky enough) to get everything else in the implementation process right, you will realise only a fraction of the true potential business benefits.

Given the main motivations of most senior executives and their chosen consultants, this sorry state of affairs is totally predictable.

Executives today are not business design specialists and many have a very limited understanding of what is possible. Therefore they are highly susceptible to business 'fashions'. Bright, shiny new ideas that promise to solve all those intransigent business problems that you never quite got to grips with can all too easily become full-blown or partial panaceas. Limited understanding leads to a lack of real scrutiny and a simplistic mindset typified by comments such as "If the XYZ corporation did it, why can't we?" And if the executive concerned happens to know the chief executive of XYZ personally and he's enthusiastic about their progress to date, so much the better. Why not talk to XYZ's consultants?

The consultants, on the other hand, typically have a particular methodology or limited set of change tools in their 'kitbag' and need to optimise their return on the particular business fashion of the moment. A minority of their people are very good indeed and are in heavy demand, typically advising lesser consultants on a variety of assignments. But from the consultancy's point of view as a business, the real money is earned by their numerous 'so-so' consultants and not by their real high flyers. So the standard, fashionable approach that sells today is key, the lowest common factor tends to dominate .... and naive executives talking of "business transformation" or "reengineering" are like manna from heaven.

The end result of this naive executive/constrained consultant 'marriage' is the 80%+ failure rule that we described earlier. Still, there is usually some limited success that can be used to cover backs all round and the executive is older, wiser and more cynical by the time the next business fashion hits the conference circuit.

But while all this is going on, the business suffers another lost opportunity to do it right. And out there, somewhere, there is another business that realises that there is a better way. There really is a combination of business design ideas that would meet your specific business needs, and not just any old businesses' needs.

In the meantime, hope and pray that those adopting the better way are not a competitor.

Ineffective change training

The third main hurdle to successful business transformation is the highly variable, and generally poor, quality of change training.

In our experience, the quality and effectiveness of the training used in major change situations depends heavily on the type of training being undertaken. We have categorised change training into two main types – 'hard' and 'soft'.

'Hard' change training covers traditional skills, such as selling, account management, contract negotiations, learning to use new IT systems, the most routine aspects of 'customer care', and so on. Generally speaking, the more specific and practical the training is, the better it is understood and translated into a new work environment. Therefore the fixed, routine elements of work (such as using a new computer system to take customer orders, or remembering to say "how can I help you" and "thank you for calling" when answering telephone enquiries) are usually tackled pretty well by traditional training methods.

In contrast, however, some of the less routine (and more important) aspects of new work environments – such as teamworking and empowerment – are often major causes of problems. And since new work environments are usually implemented initially on a limited scale to check out viability, more extensive use of new approaches can be severely delayed or cancelled altogether.

The use of unimaginative, formal training to deal with these 'soft' training needs often generates more confusion than it removes. In some of the worst cases we have come across, formal classroom-style training is given to a wide variety of staff, who are then expected to translate the theory and enthusiasm of the presenters into real-world actions and team relationships. The results are often chaotic and demoralising. Repeats of the key formal training elements in an attempt to solve the resulting problems will usually only make things worse.

At the other end of the spectrum, however, a minority of soft change training is done very well indeed. Imaginative, largely informal training, based on team workshops that simulate different aspects of new work environments have been used to great effect. We have been particularly pleased with the results of repeated team workshops that take place both before and after a major change, and gradually reduce in frequency as experience of the new work situation builds up.

So, in summary, hard change training is generally at an acceptable standard – provided you choose competent training suppliers. But the standard of soft change training is generally abysmal. Go for imaginative training suppliers, who advocate the workshop/new world simulation approach and involve all the relevant people in new work discussions, even if these are sometimes outside the scope of individuals' current roles. And don't skimp on the number or variety of workshops. A few pennies saved on soft training today will lose you many pounds in chaos and confusion tomorrow. Or worse still, it will stop you gaining the benefits of well-thought-through new business designs.

'Lethargic' IT systems

We regard 'lethargic' IT systems as potentially the least important of the four main hurdles, but one that nevertheless has played a significant part in disrupting many of the change initiatives that we investigated.

The reasons for these problems are numerous and often technical, but from a business design perspective are quite easy to understand. Many business process redesign exercises involve moving away from traditional, separate, functional IT systems to multifunctional, integrated systems that support a range of tasks across traditional functional boundaries. To compound the problems of achieving this 'horizontal' linkage, most of the old functional systems were not designed to work in this way, nor were these systems designed for flexibility or ease of change.

IT staff are therefore often torn between doing a 'quick and dirty' job that will require lots of ongoing modifications and support, and spending an unacceptably long time rewriting several large and complex application systems.

Fortunately, the IT community is beginning to learn from its early mistakes in building horizontal systems. This gradual enlightenment is being supported by increasing maturity in several of the key enabling technologies and approaches, notably client-server technology and rapid application development approaches. Looking ahead to the early years of the new millennium, we predict that the next major breakthrough in IT technology (standard, but highly flexible, system modules called 'objects') will be nearing maturity.

However, in the meantime the best IT people will strike an appropriate and pragmatic balance between timescales and system resilience, making the best use of the tools and approaches available.

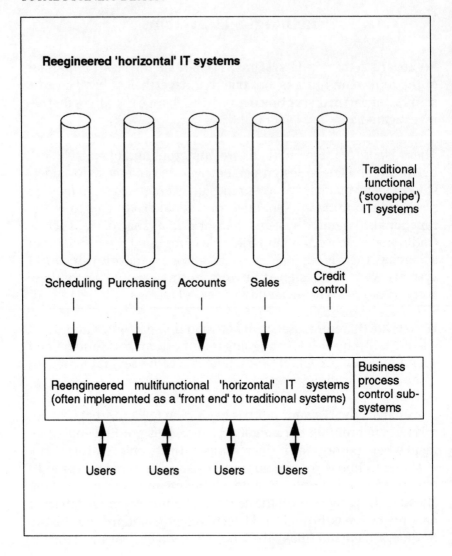

~ 6 ~
Ideas that break the mould

As the impact of Japanese and other developing world competition began to be appreciated fully during the 1980s, Western businesses desperately sought new and more effective ways of running their operations.

A whole raft of new (and revamped) business ideas came into vogue. These ranged from traditional downsizing and other forms of cost cutting, through core business concepts and strategic alliances, to borrowing Japanese quality approaches and inventing 'business process reengineering'.

Some of these ideas came in bundled groupings of tenuously related ideas that were marketed by gurus and other consultants under brand names, such as TQM and Business Process Reengineering. The quality movement, for example, often encompassed the concepts of 'continuous improvement', 'right first time every time', statistical sampling, customer care and strategic alliances with suppliers. Similarly, business process reengineering concentrated on process redesign, multiskilling, empowerment, teamwork, and flattened organisational structures.

While each of these two combinations can be justified from the narrow perspective of their origins – largely one man's view of quality (Dr Deming) and a sponsored MIT survey into alternatives to functional hierarchies – we believe that the time has come to broaden our perspectives.

In the remainder of this section on 'ideas that break the mould' we therefore describe briefly some of the main underlying business design approaches that have been influential in recent years .... removing them from their brand labels.

In each case, we highlight the main benefits of the design and its most apparent limitations.

As we expand on the concept of Total Business Design in the later sections of this book, we explain why different businesses will require different combinations of these 'ideas that break the mould' if they are to optimise their business designs over time. (For those in a hurry, skip through to Section 7.)

Core business concepts

During the 1980s and early 1990s, the concept of rationalising businesses down to their core, essential business elements came into vogue.

Historical analysis of the performance of conglomerate-style business groups led many business leaders to the conclusion that business success was closely correlated with concentrating on "what we do best". Over the last decade, pharmaceutical companies have sold their medical instrument divisions, retailers have sold many of their overseas stores, builders concentrated on building things rather than owning builders' merchants, city finance houses cut back on unprofitable fringe operations, and privatised utilities sought ways to exploit their core skills while avoiding the inhibiting scrutiny of their respective industry regulators. Very few executives tried to mimic the great diverse business builders, such as Hanson and White.

While many of these moves to core businesses were well thought through, there is little doubt that many others were based on highly superficial, almost knee jerk, reactions to adverse economic conditions. Many learnt the harsh lesson that just because you are quite good at manufacturing products in the UK, it does not necessarily follow that this success can be repeated abroad. And while you may have a good reputation for quality and service in one market, it can be fatal to assume that you can build this afresh in a very different competitive environment. What you thought of as your core business competencies may not be your real strengths at all. And your perceptions of core business elements may really be built on sand.

Gradually, we learnt that the concept of core business is not always easy and we sought guidance from academic and other researchers. What, we asked, are the real rules of the core business game?

Of the many reports and books published to guide executives on identifying core businesses in the real world, we have chosen an approach developed by John Kay of the London Business School as being the most useful in practice. Like many good ideas, this approach has the twin advantages of being built on a wide range of practical experiences, while at the same time being quite simple and easy to use.

Kay's approach is based on the premise that sustainable competitive advantage that generates added value to a business over a significant period of time can only be achieved where:

"distinctive capabilities are applied effectively in appropriate markets".

In Kay's model, there are four, and only four, distinctive capabilities .... innovation, architecture, reputation and strategic assets.

Innovation usually relates to distinctive properties in a business's products or services. And indeed some organisations have gained massively from specific innovative products. For example, Glaxo became one of the largest multinational businesses in the world during the 1980s, largely due to the development of the stomach ulcer drug Zantac, which generated many billions of pounds of revenue for the company.

However, it is more frequently an organisation's ability to continually produce innovative products or services that leads to real business value added in the medium and long term. It is important to recognise that what may appear to be the business rewards of a particular innovation, may in reality reflect either a particular stroke of one-off luck or a more profound and ongoing capability to develop innovative products and services. Most research-based companies, for example, have set up their R&D establishments with the objective of producing a steady stream of new innovations. Other businesses have specialised in creating marketing mechanisms that enable them to sell a variety of new innovations very effectively into their chosen markets. New innovations that cannot be exploited effectively are of little business value.

Architecture is a term used to describe the inherent ability to generate and/or exploit business opportunities. In reality, architecture usually refers to the nature of business relationships that have been established or to the 'knowledge' held within a particular business.

Relationships may be internal (where, for example, a particularly effective design team has been established) or external (where strong strategic supplier relationships have been forged or where very effective local sales teams have close links with the customer base).

Business knowledge is a less tangible architectural asset that often underpins new product developments or new ways of exploiting particular markets. For example, knowledge of customer complaints about existing products will often lead to better new product offerings; and knowledge of distributor capabilities may enable the company to respond rapidly once a new distribution opportunity becomes available.

Reputation is usually created in a specific market, although on occasions a very strong and widely understood reputation can be used as a basis for building business in new market areas. One of the most notable examples of exploiting reputation in recent years is Richard Branson's 'Virgin'. Although Virgin's reputation is strongly entwined with the personal charisma and exploits of Branson himself, they have been remarkably successful in developing this somewhat idiosyncratic reputation into one representing fair dealing and value for money. In taking on major players in a variety of different markets (British Airways, Coca Cola and the big insurance companies), Virgin is now clearly following a reputation-based marketing strategy – in effect, they are saying:

"Trust us. We will treat you fairly and give you good value ....
(by implication) in contrast to those other 'fat cats'."

In many respects, this type of marketing-based strategy breaks all the superficial rules of core business concepts. After all, which other senior business executive would seriously argue that their core business comprised an international airline, a marketer of cola-type products, and a provider of investment products? Yet, from a strong reputation platform, Branson's core business approach is entirely logical and quite compelling.

Strategic assets are the final type of distinctive capability identified by John Kay. The most obvious type of strategic asset is a natural monopoly. Natural monopolies can result from economies of scale or from narrow markets. For example, many would argue that the supply of infrastructure services, such as power cables, railway lines, and the sewage system were all natural monopolies. While secondary suppliers may well pay to use these natural monopoly services, there is no real business case for duplicating these facilities on any scale.

A second type of strategic asset exists where very large capital investments have been made in the past to create a capability that, although not a natural monopoly, inhibits new players from entering a particular market. Large building firms with major land banks in a particular area fall into this category, as do big engineering companies specialising in large capital projects, such as submarines or power stations.

Strategic assets may also result from other circumstances, including the granting of licences to operate in specific business areas, such as patents on particular products; franchises at airports; licences to run telecommunication services; or airline routes.

In Kay's model, any combination of these four distinctive capabilities – innovation, architecture, reputation and strategic assets – can be used to create competitive advantage in appropriate markets. Where competitive advantage is sustainable and where the business concerned is able to extract the benefits from this advantage (and not be forced to give most of the margins to third parties, such as governments, for instance) then the business will be able to enjoy added value over a period of time.

The Kay model of core business concepts puts us in a position to remove the blinkers traditionally associated with core businesses. The underlying logic is powerful and easy to understand, and fits well with other 'ideas that break the mould', such as business process redesign and strategic alliances. Using the model is just a matter of challenging all your long-held assumptions on what your core business really is. What are your real business innovations?

Which elements of your business infrastructure are really strong in relation to existing and potential competitors? How strong is your current business reputation, with which community and in which geographic areas? Do you have any realisable strategic assets and what is the likely future for these? Are any new strategic assets likely to come up for grabs in future? How strong is your total combination of distinctive capabilities and how can you maximise the impact on business value added in the short, medium and long term?

The Kay model is a useful starting point for any Total Business Design exercise.

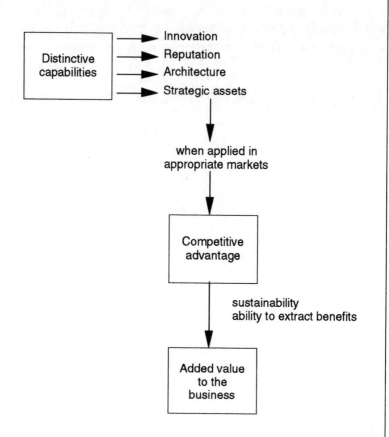

Designing your 'core' business elements

Distinctive capabilities
- Innovation
- Reputation
- Architecture
- Strategic assets

when applied in appropriate markets

Competitive advantage

sustainability
ability to extract benefits

Added value to the business

Source: Modified from John Kay, London Business School

Experience 1: Core business concepts

Marks and Spencer plc

To illustrate John Kay's approach to identifying core business elements, we look at the case of Marks and Spencer, one of the UK's most well-known modern companies.

During the 1970s and 1980s, Marks and Spencer was one of Europe's leading companies. Halfway through the 1990s, the company has maintained its position in the retail market and has, at great risk to its standing as a quality clothing and food retailer, successfully expanded into the financial markets with the introduction of financial products including unit trusts. These changes were achieved with a low-profile advertising and marketing campaign.

Marks and Spencer's position as a leading retail outlet has almost been taken for granted in the last three decades, but even for a company with an enviable reputation for quality, reliability and to some extent, value, success in the financial sector was not assured. Nevertheless, the unit trust launch in 1988 attracted £56 million, a substantial sum, which was almost certainly down to the company's existing reputation. Despite the undeniable part that reputation played in the success, the Marks and Spencer case illustrates the necessary combination of distinctive capabilities required to duplicate success across varying business activities.

There can be few companies in the UK with a more prestigious reputation than Marks and Spencer. The company has forged such a relationship with its customers (one recently published women's magazine claimed that a third of all its readers would be wearing Marks and Spencer underwear!) that it is tempting to attribute its success to this factor alone   This is not the case. Marks and Spencer is just as reliant on its internal architecture (the relationship built up between the company and its employees) and with the contracts it has developed with carefully selected suppliers (the external architecture).

Indeed, it is the network of high-quality suppliers that has enabled Marks and Spencer to retain such a high regard in its markets and in particular develop a further enhanced reputation for quality food

.../cont'd

provision. Kay describes these relationships between Marks and Spencer and the chosen suppliers as 'relational contracts'. The suppliers commit a major portion of their output to Marks and Spencer and are closely monitored throughout their provision of goods and services. Many have been informal partners for decades and, in some cases, are almost entirely dependent on their business with the retailer.

What this illustrates is that the company has built internal and external architectures that at first established, and then later supported, a strong reputation for certain qualities. A good reputation, which has taken many years to cultivate, can be damaged in an instant (think of Gerald Ratner) and it requires more than a few satisfied customers to gain such a reputation. Marks and Spencer knew this when crafting their business strategy and installed the appropriate architecture to stand them in good stead for changes in fashion, buying preference and competition. Yet competitive advantage based on architecture can be diminished also and it takes careful adaptation for a period of dominance to last over a number of decades. So it is the distinctive capability of the Marks and Spencer architecture, combined with a vigorously exploited reputation (and the ability to apparently transfer that reputation across sectors), that has led to continued success.

Core employee concepts/outsourcing

Once the scope and stability of the core business elements have been determined, the next logical stage in examining the total design of a business is to consider which activities should be carried out internally by employees, and which can be outsourced to a greater or lesser degree.

Many household name businesses are made up of an 'image shell' that covers a variety of outsourcing arrangements, with many of the business activities being carried out by organisations that few people have ever heard of. Marks and Spencer do not make their own clothes or foods; Benetton is an Italian-owned franchise image and marketing operation that makes virtually nothing and owns fewer than ten of its branded stores; own-brand supermarket products are almost universally made by other manufacturers, many of whom produce competitive brands; and several well-known petroleum companies neither extract oil, nor refine petrol.

In carrying out the core employee/outsourcing elements of Total Business Design exercises, we have been strongly influenced by the early work of Charles Handy and, in particular, his concept of the 'Shamrock Organisation' described in his book "The Age of Unreason', published in 1989. Handy's 'shamrock' business organisation is made up of three main types of people:

- *Core workers,* who are the people that are essential to the organisation and its success. Increasingly, these will be qualified professionals, technicians and managers/team leaders. Many of these core workers will exhibit strong teamworking and multiskilled capabilities, with high levels of initiative and flexibility being commonplace. Businesses will increasingly value these workers and bind them with what Handy calls 'hoops of gold' .... high salaries, fringe benefits, lots of training and company cars. In return, the organisation will demand hard work and long hours, commitment and flexibility.

- *Part-time workers,* who make up a highly flexible additional pool of resource to cope with peaks in workload, without incurring the traditional disruption associated with temporary staff who are not suitably trained or familiar with the work that needs to be done. As Handy says "It is cheaper by far, though more trouble, to bring in occasional extra labour part time, to cope with extra hours, or temporary, to cope with peak periods. Convenience for the management has been weighed against economy and economy has won." In designing organisations to make optimal use of part time workers, a balance needs to be struck between providing guaranteed levels of work, necessary training provision, and costs.

- *Outsource workers*, who carry out all non-essential or 'commodity' type work. As Handy says "All non-essential work, work which could be done by someone else, is sensibly contracted out to people who make a speciality of it and who should, in theory, be able to do it better for less cost ...." In practice outsourcing carries a significant control overhead if the outsource suppliers are not to dominate the relationship. As a rule of thumb, we have found that "never outsource your strategy, nor your ability to innovate in important business areas" tempers many overheated outsourcing proposals. Nevertheless, outsourcing can be highly effective in the right circumstances .... both for strategic long-term outsourcing (where the activities are truly commodity in nature) and for shorter-term tactical purposes (where poorly performing internal units can be disposed of/re-invigorated by a period of outsourcing).

When a Total Business Design exercise leads to major changes in the types of workers that will be needed in future, the transition process usually represents a real challenge if major morale and operational disruptions are to be avoided.

Experience 2: Core employee concepts/Outsourcing

F International

The British company F International (FI) is a true shamrock organisation that has blossomed from humble beginnings as Freelance Programmers (the 'F' in FI) in 1962 to FI in 1964, then onto the FI Group in 1988. The company has in excess of 1,100 staff and a turnover of some £20 million. It is also worth study because of its owner's obsession with flexibility and empowering workers through employee ownership schemes.

Mrs 'Steve' Shirley first ran Freelance Programmers from her own home to tap into the supply of freelance computer workers, most of whom also worked at home. The company is unusual in that it was not 'forced' to transform into a shamrock in order to survive, since it was formed along those lines from the outset. Equally unusual is the considerable success FI has had in keeping its form over many years of growth. The company represents an extreme example, but shows how it is possible to formulate a defined strategy for worker retention and rotation.

FI has a small number of core staff at its Head Office, a few branch offices, and in recent years has been keen to develop a network of cost-effective 'work centres' where people can choose to work if they wish and use specialist equipment. Home workers are kept in touch using e-Mail, 'phone/fax lines and PCs, and by attending 'free speaks' where core workers hold open question-and-answer sessions.

Approximately 90% of FI workers are women. Most are self-employed, work part-time and at home. If they can guarantee a certain amount of commitment to FI, they can go onto a payroll, although by the end of 1994, less than 300 had done so.

These 'part-time workers' (the second of Handy's personnel classifications) do not work in isolation, but 'band' together in teams for specific and often relatively short-lived projects. Many of the female workers have young families, so this type of unconventional structure is ideal for their life-style. Steve Shirley believes that FI workers'

.../cont'd

performance is approximately 30% higher than the competition whose staff are interrupted by coffee breaks, informal chats and gossiping. FI has a symbiotic relationship with its staff and realises that the company structure is not 'bullet proof'. The company invests a great deal of time in training its workers, in listening to their needs and in fostering strong communication links. FI endeavours to provide a competitive wage.

With such a dynamic and constantly changing pool of workers, FI has had to be acutely aware of the difficulties of maintaining high levels of performance and morale. Investing in training, providing good financial incentives and encouraging communication has helped, but the founder was keen to develop and nurture a real sense of ownership amongst employees. This vision of participation was transformed into action in the early 1980s, when Shirley distributed shares via two schemes: one by rights (reflecting service and commitment) and the other by gifts (individual achievements and team performance) until 24% of FI was employee owned.

The scheme was not sufficient enough to create a real feeling of ownership amongst employees, perhaps because over three-quarters of the company shares remained with the founder. (Our research shows that token efforts of this sort are likely to produce only limited success.) FI saw this and made radical changes to their plans, not least of which was the appointment of Peter Thompson as the new chairman, fresh from his successes with The National Freight Corporation.

Thompson initiated a share transfer scheme that heavily increased employee and associate ownership percentages. By 1995, some 80% of FI staff owned shares. The company is expected to be floated during 1996, with a stock market value of about £70 million.

Planning people numbers and competencies

In recent years, the concept of strategic planning has gone seriously out of fashion. After all, with businesses changing at unprecedented rates, most executives can't see much beyond the end of the current year, let alone three or five years ahead. Those who spend their time in ivory towers contemplating future business strategies are largely wasting their time and (since they represent considerable overhead costs in hard economic times) they really have to go!

We believe there is some truth in this argument, but that a 'plan nothing' extreme in turbulent times is potentially fatal.

In carrying out a Total Business Design exercise on future people requirements, we need to clarify both who is responsible for these projections and the resulting actions, and how the planning work itself should be done.

The 'who is responsible' question is easy to answer. The senior executive team is responsible, not some staff function, such as human resources or corporate planning. A small specialist team may carry out some of the mechanics of such an exercise (or external consultants may be used as guides and facilitators) but the isolated human resource/corporate planning specialists baffling executives with the latest technospeak is doomed to fail. In planning people numbers and competencies in a rapidly changing world, commitment and real understanding by the senior executive team is mandatory.

The 'how do we do the planning' question is also easy to answer, although most organisations fall into the overcomplexity trap and fail to adopt an obvious, pragmatic and effective approach. The first rule of thumb for strategic planning is that the results are only valuable if we do something different as a result .... this year! It's an obvious rule but one that is almost universally overlooked.

In carrying out the people planning exercise we therefore need to identify the most likely major business scenarios (say) three to five years ahead, and then work out whether these business alternatives

31

will have a significantly different people numbers/competencies requirement. Usually, we find that many of the people requirements are common across the (typically) two or three realistic business scenarios being considered. However, where there are significant differences, some will be low risk (even if we get it wrong, we can fill the gap relatively easily through recruitment or subcontract) and others high risk (if we get it wrong we will be missing some key resources that could delay actions in key business areas and badly affect the bottom line). In practice, senior executive effort is only really justified in planning the tactics necessary to minimise risk in these high-risk areas. This approach minimises effort, focuses minds wonderfully and is very effective.

When you carry out an exercise of this type, we recommend taking one year 'snapshots' of each major scenario out to three, four or five years ahead. In this way, you will be able to identify new options that become realistic over time and to progressively translate these into rough people requirements in each case. The people requirements picture is reviewed annually and adjusted as necessary. But always remember that the real benefits of this exercise lie in what you do differently this year – recruiting different types of people, not recruiting others, changing contracts of employment for core staff, part-time staff and outsourced people, and so on.

The documentation generated by this people planning exercise will contain details of people number requirements by competency over time. Although a lot of words and hot air have been generated on the subject of competencies in recent years, we have adopted a simple competency categorisation based on:

- *Skills*, primarily technical-type skills.

- *Knowledge*, of particular key aspects of the business or its competitive environment.

- *Behaviours*, such as teamworking characteristics, innovative drives or leadership qualities.

In carrying out people planning, we have found that people numbers and skills are the main outputs. When the resulting actions are initiated, such as the recruitment of new people or the transfer of staff to different positions, then knowledge and behaviour characteristics need to be fleshed out. (Doing the detailed competency analysis at an earlier stage just wastes time and effort.)

By the way, identifying the behaviours of people is a far from simple task and most organisations that are driven by the latest 'competencies' fashion get it quite badly wrong.

The people/competency planning cone

Scenario 1   Scenario 2

Implications for today

Common short-term actions
+
Different short-term actions (low risk)
+
Different short-term actions (high risk)

Focus on high-risk short-term actions

Short- and medium-term transition plans

◯ Possible options in each time period

◍ Likely practical options in each time period

Experience 3: Planning people competencies

Safeway plc

Safeway, the retail food outlet, has been committed to the use of a 'competency framework' for the selection, assessment and development of staff for over a decade. In 1985, the company opened a Retail Career Development Centre (RCDC) and is the principal supporter of the Management Charter Initiative (MCI), which was launched in 1989 to improve management awareness of development issues. The MCI was developed specifically around a competence approach to employee selection and development.

The RCDC is a progressive approach to training and developing employees and their skills. The UK centre was 'copied' from Safeway's one-time US parent company and proved to be an instant success. The key to its success lies in the environment that employees are assessed in. The centre aims to establish the necessary competencies that are required to effectively perform as a store manager, and existing staff are assessed in 'simulated' store management settings, to gauge their effectiveness within a relevant context.

The success of the RCDC prompted Safeway to establish a requisite set of competencies for their employees, which they consequently established company wide. The competency framework has been used across most aspects of management recruitment, so that it now includes graduate selection and employee career and development planning.

The approach to competency evaluation is based on a hierarchy of competency classification. There are three levels to this. The first, 'major competence', describes the general areas of operation in which Safeway managers are expected to be proficient. These include managing resources and job-specific professional competencies. Each of the four major competencies have twelve sub 'core competencies' that constitute the majority of the skills that employees will need. These particular areas of personal competence cover issues as wide ranging as 'problem solving' and 'stress tolerance'. The third level of classification is 'competencies' which represent combinations of core competencies that have further elements of

.../cont'd

specific skill and knowledge. For example the 'competence' might be to 'monitor and maintain all cash-handling procedures' for which the required combination of 'core competencies' would be 'problems analysis', 'problem solving' and 'management control'. This wide ranging set of competencies is tuned for individual jobs in terms of specific required performance criteria. For the example competence given above, 'monitor and maintain all cash-handling procedures', one performance criterion would be to 'complete weekly cash results for the area manager'.

This approach has been adopted by Safeway with regard to its existing employees and is used when recruiting new staff, for example in the case of graduate intake. A graduate management trainee works in several different stores while performing a selection of functions. As the person's career develops, s/he is given a series of management assignments mixed in with off-the-job training specifically designed to develop the competencies that were specified exactly by Safeway in their competency classification. Following five successful years of this technique, the trainee is assessed at the RCDC. This ensures that all gaps in development are filled and the graduate can expect to receive the MCI Diploma in Management studies when s/he has demonstrated a sufficient knowledge and practice of the required Safeway competencies.

While it is accepted that many changes will occur in the period that employees are assessed against the Safeway competence 'set', and although the competence classification remains intact, the beauty of this system lies in its inherent flexibility. The ability to modify the scenario settings against which candidates are tested enables Safeway to respond to changing circumstances when planning its development of existing employees, and the selection of those that will meet future requirements.

Business process redesign

The breakthrough idea behind business process redesign is that it rejects the conventional wisdom of functional hierarchies. Once this sacred cow has been slaughtered, we are free to reconsider almost all traditional design criteria for the business machine.

A change of this type and potential magnitude generates a great deal of fear. It has radical implications for the career paths of some very influential people within any business. This combination of huge business potential and fear amongst the 'movers and shakers' has contributed significantly to disillusion about 'business process reengineering' in general.

However, before we can consign process redesign to the file marked 'yet another over-hyped idea', we must reflect on the real potential and constraints of this approach. If we take the logic of process redesign to its ultimate conclusion, we often end up with an organisational structure similar to that illustrated in the figure overleaf.

In this arrangement, most of the people remaining in the business after the redesign has been implemented will work in teams dealing with particular business products or services.

These product/service teams will be supported conceptually by a multifaceted 'system' that is designed to optimise the efficiency of all the processes associated with (for example) purchasing, modifying and selling a particular product, as well as paying bills, collecting money and accounting for all the financial transactions. In reality, this support system will become more integrated, flexible, sophisticated and proactive over time as the underlying software matures. (It will then become a viable replacement for the missing tiers of supervisors and middle managers that have long since departed, usually amid some chaos.)

In this new arrangement, we will require very few specialists as they used to exist in the old functional organisation. For instance, purchasing will be initiated almost universally by the relevant

Process redesign: the ultimate conclusion

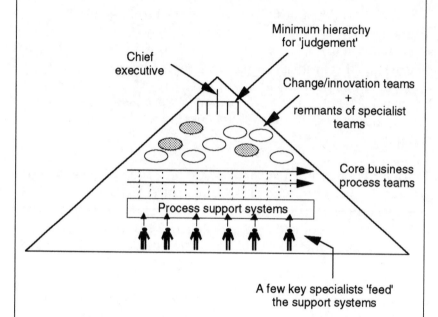

Note: 'Virtual' team that is disbanded once a particular project is completed

'Permanent' team that continues to carry out specialist tasks, such as R&D, marketing, etc.

Note: It has become fashionable in recent years to invert the traditional organisational triangle, to stress that all employees should support those at the customer interface. We believe that this inversion is fallacious, since it ignores major changes due to revised business designs.

product/service team and the number of specialist 'purchasers' required to support the non-routine purchasing part of the 'system' will be very few indeed. As this type of arrangement matures, we might even expect that the role of specialist purchaser (negotiating new call-off contracts for raw materials etc) might well be undertaken by a member of the relevant product/service team. This will be particularly true as well-designed multiskilling within these teams becomes the norm rather than the exception.

These multiskilled individuals will have a much wider scope of job responsibility than was traditionally the case in functional hierarchies. Job rotation within teams will be encouraged to ensure that a wide range of relevant skills are available in a variety of combinations. At the extreme, we will be seriously questioning the need for any support services that directly relate to the processes of carrying out day-to-day business activities. In other words, people whose jobs used to be in purchasing, administrative support, personnel, IT, accounts and other traditional support areas will now often work directly within product/service teams.

All employees, however, will not work in these process teams. The logic of process redesign leads to the conclusion that there will be at least three further types of employee within the new business organisation.

The second type of employee are those whose jobs relate primarily to major changes in the business. For example, those working in R&D, or those concerned with getting a new product or service to market. While some of these individuals will also have roles within the day-to-day product/service teams, we believe that process redesign will eventually stabilise around a small number of new development teams working alongside the various product/service teams. This type of employee will frequently be involved in project work, where individuals are chosen to work on particular projects because of their skills, knowledge and behaviours (a combination often called 'competencies'). Some early redesign exercises have led to employees of this type being organised into resource pools of specialists or generalists, with their value to the business being indicated by the percentage of their time that they are chosen to work on meaningful projects.

39

The third type of people working within this redesigned organisation will be those who represent the remains of the functional hierarchy. We believe that these individuals will exert the ultimate judgement in terms of new policies and new developments in the business.

There will also usually be a chief executive .... the fourth type of employee, who will coordinate the business vision and break deadlocks at the level-three 'directors'.

The design rationale behind this judgement is that teams are usually better at carrying out a series of process tasks and at developing individual inspirations into new business ideas. However, in many cases, individuals are better at solving specific day-to-day problems and at making timely judgements. This latter requirement we believe is key to getting the right balance between individual empowerment, team work and the necessary functional hierarchy in redesigned new business organisations.

Four types of work: Individual or team?

Type of work	Best done by:	Individual ——⟋⟍—— Team balances
• Judgement	Individual	⟋⟍
• Problem solving	Individual/Team	⟋⟍
• Creative	Team	⟋⟍
• Process	Team	⟋⟍

Note: The 'best' approaches shown in this figure represent balances between those situations where individuals are 'best' at doing the work and where teams are 'best'.

The impact of this redesign approach will be radical, and often traumatic, in traditional large bureaucratic organisations. In organisations of this type, we quite commonly see a potential to reduce administrative and management numbers by more than 50% .... and in some cases by more than 70%. However, in smaller, leaner organisations the potential for staff savings due to process redesign is much more limited. Many smaller organisations that have attempted process redesign have been disappointed at the overall potential for staff cost savings, often representing 10% or less of the total wage bill. The reason for this is very straightforward. There is a lower limit to the degree to which multifunction teams can operate efficiently when compared to lean functional units. There just is not the surplus fat to be removed. Changing fundamental business cultures and personal aspirations is a costly exercise, and where the potential benefits are small the law of diminishing returns applies with a vengeance.

In setting up the Total Business Design model, we have included these and other considerations relating to the scope and potential for process redesign.

In summary, process redesign will usually lead to the following four main organisational elements:

- A relatively large tier consisting of process workers dealing with day-to-day product/service activities.

- Typically smaller teams dealing with major changes to business products or business structure/activities. Some of these teams will be permanent, for example in the R&D area, while others will be transitory, for example in a task force looking at new ways to sell existing products. The trend is towards transitory teams.

- A minimal executive hierarchy, into which the team leaders in the above two categories will typically report.

- A chief executive.

Although much process redesign up to now has concentrated on cost reduction and elapsed-time reduction in meeting customer needs, we believe that the potential for process redesign is much greater than these initial objectives. In particular, multiskilled, flexible individuals at key points in the organisation have the potential to handle a rapidly changing business environment much more swiftly and effectively than when they worked in traditional functional units.

In this new organisational environment there will often be a high level of outsourcing of non-core activities.

So if these and other related redesign concepts are well understood by most reengineering consultants, why are the failure rates so high? The answer lies in the design balance and the timing of implementation, and is governed by a very different set of change management criteria.

Experience 4: Business Process Redesign

Taco Bell

The Taco Bell case illustrates all that is good and bad about business process redesign efforts. Michael Hammer and James Champy of 'Reengineering the corporation' fame, tell the story of the Mexican fast-food chain store that, by 1983, was "sick and getting sicker". The newly appointed CEO, John Martin, was handed the job of revitalising the company, in what at the time was a diminishing market. According to Hammer and Champy, the exercise was a complete success and stood as one of the best examples of a successful reengineering effort. The authors enthused in their book:

> "John Martin's story is inspiring. His reengineering effort paid off magnificently as Taco Bell's sales soared from $500 million to $3 billion in an industry that is declining."

So from this description, and when exploring the details of such a seemingly successful reengineering initiative, we should expect to find nothing less than an uplifting tale of business transformation against all the odds, with success that has endured up until the present time. This is not exactly the case. But first we shall look at the more encouraging aspects of the Taco Bell experience and in particular, a number of redesign steps that were successful ......

The single most important aspect of the Taco Bell partial revival was the total focus on the customer. Customer numbers had been steadily dwindling for several years and it was the stark realisation that this was likely to accelerate rather than abate, that first spurred management into action, with the appointment of John Martin. Taco Bell had a classical management organisational structure with numerous levels of management sorting, processing and passing paper, but doing little else of real value. The company was so tied up with the 'process of processing' that it neglected the most important issue for a food retailer of its type – what the customer really wanted.

Martin knew this and set about forging a vision, something that would inspire the management and the workers to transform the

.../cont'd

company into "a giant in the fast food industry". This was ambitious, as between 1978 and 1982 cumulative growth for Taco Bell stood at negative 16% compared to the total industry's positive 6%.

Martin discovered that, by asking the customers what they really required, the company did not have such a hard task on its hands. Customer requirements were relatively simple ; good food, served fast, in a clean environment and at a price they could afford. Taco Bell initiated a reengineering programme that would be firmly focused on meeting those requirements – and nothing else. The company decided to reduce everything, except the cost of goods sold. Layers of management were eliminated, nearly every job was redefined and local restaurant owners were given considerable autonomy to account for their own restaurants. Some 100 managers controlled 2,300 restaurants; previously there had been 350 managers in control of 1,800 restaurants. Fundamental changes were introduced that saw a switch from 70% of the restaurant being kitchen space and 30% for customers to the exact reverse.

A resounding success? At first. Profit growth has averaged increases of 31% since 1989, sales have increased 22% and transaction numbers are up considerably. John Martin summed up his company's reengineering effort at the time, with this :

"For us, the process of reengineering has been like a voyage of discovery – a voyage we have been on now for nearly a decade, and one that we realise will continue as long as Taco Bell is in the business of serving customers."

However, following the Hammer and Champy coverage, Datamation magazine reported on a follow-up reengineering project at Taco Bell that went badly wrong. In the summer of 1994, the magazine reported on the disaster of a copy-cat reengineering effort that attempted to emulate previous success, this time for the opening of new restaurants, leading with the headline : "Taco Bell BPR project hits clanger."

The reasons for failure, according to Taco Bell's Information Systems vice president, Susan Cramm, sound all too familiar. The project was abandoned because of a lack of real commitment from

.../cont'd

the board and a hazy, incoherent vision that failed to focus on delivering customer value. (These, and other main reasons for failures in transformation exercises are covered in Section 5.)

The final irony in the story? The problem project was assisted by CSC Index, reengineering specialists, whose chairman happens to be one James Champy.

Empowerment

A natural extension of the design logic in business process redesign is that teams should have much increased responsibilities (only rarely needing to refer upwards for authorisation) and that many individuals should be similarly 'empowered'. After all, the supervisors and middle managers who used to take many semi-routine decisions are just not there any more.

In theory, teams must be self managed to a high degree because it is the people doing the job who know best how to change and improve their own and the company's performance, and they should therefore be given the authority to do so. The leading quality guru, Dr Deming, estimated that in traditional hierarchies perhaps 10% of hourly paid workers and 2% of middle management really enjoyed their work. Academics have argued for decades that we are underutilising the potential of our workforces to a scandalous degree. More recently, high-profile gurus like Tom Peters have shouted this message from hundreds of public platforms on the conference circuit.

But, while the theory behind empowerment is compelling, the realities are often more complex and less satisfactory.

The story of the Federal Express employee in North America who, on his own initiative, chartered a helicopter to deliver a package to a snowed-in mountain home has become legendary. But in this one example we can readily identify both the potential impact of employee empowerment and some very real dangers.

In reality, the transition from traditional hierarchies to empowered individuals within self-managed teams has proved to be far from easy. Indeed, it is in the broad area of empowerment that we have found the greatest degree of confusion and uncertainty. Business executives, not surprisingly, blanch visibly when presented with examples of radical empowerment like that at Federal Express. "Where do we really draw the line?" they ask. "Do we really want our salespeople and order clerks promising to remedy all customer grievances, irrespective of cost and setting precedents for the future?" In short, many executives wonder if the whole concept of empowerment is just a disaster waiting to happen.

The answer to these concerns is very simple. Where the business design has been carried out in a superficial, inadequate or incompetent way the answer is a resounding 'yes'. These are powerful concepts with major potential benefits and big risks. (Fortunately, many examples of poorly designed organisational units change as a result of minor disasters, rather than major ones. Those responsible often survive to try again – or to resist the attempts of others to change the work environment.)

However, where the business design has been well thought through and competently implemented, the dangers are certainly no greater than those associated with traditional functional hierarchies .... delays, customer dissatisfaction, "it's not my responsibility" attitudes, and so on.

Many good self-managed teams and empowered individuals do exist. They exist in conditions where the individuals concerned are very clear as to the boundaries of empowerment (which are typically much wider than with traditional functional groups, but are certainly not infinite).

Often these teams illustrate a kind of 'learning in action' that blends hunches, reflection, analysis, experimentation, adjustment, measurement and gut feel in the real-time pursuit of well-defined goals. New ideas are simulated in occasional workshops where all the potential problems (both procedural and personal) are fully explored and solutions reached. No-one is kept in the dark.

In the best teams, the boundaries of empowerment are set by a clear understanding of goals in a clear business perspective, rather than by formal role definitions or work procedures.

Empowered individuals working in self-managed teams are usually most effective where team members have a knowledge of all or many of the components of the tasks that the team is required to complete. The benefits resulting from this approach include work flexibility, team cohesiveness and individual job satisfaction/motivation. Typically, successful reward systems are designed to recognise multiskilling achievements.

Our research has shown that one of the major problem areas in developing new work environments of this type is that traditional training and education is totally inadequate. To date, the development of self-managed teams/empowered individuals has a sorry track record similar to other aspects of business transformation.

Experience 5: Empowerment

Baxi Partnership

In 1989, a new CEO joined Baxi, an old-established Preston firm of domestic boiler and heating manufacturers. He observed a company in the middle of a seemingly successful transformation from family firm to share-owning partnership. However, hidden underneath the optimism held for these changes was a catalogue of problems waiting to explode – slowdown of market growth, rising costs and changes among both competitors and customers that threatened Baxi's market share and profit margins.

Baxi had attempted to introduce worker empowerment in the late 1980s with the aim of bringing their manufacturing operations up to their competitors' level. A number of early successes were achieved with the use of empowered teams. However, towards the end of 1989 the deeper underlying problems associated with the organisational structure, coupled with a increasing disillusion at the lack of widespread success, caused the effort to flounder. The embedded hierarchical function-based structure was smothering suggestions from the teams, alienating the participating members and limiting visible success.

This is typical of the problems associated with moving away from traditional hierarchy towards self-managed teams and true individual empowerment. What was really needed, above and beyond shallow notions of 'empowered workers', was a wholesale restructuring of the business design. In January of 1990, this is what Baxi undertook. The new CEO initiated a radical revamp of the functional 'chimneys' that was to reverberate throughout the company.

First, the company was divided into six self-governing business areas with some activities retained as central services. The resulting organisational structure resembled a wheel, with the board in the centre, surrounded by business area managers and an outer layer of team leaders. The idea of the 'wheel' was to emphasise the holistic nature of the business, where no job was more or less important than any other, and all were seen to be interdependent. The directors abandoned their old and dated responsibilities for functions such as marketing and sales, instead holding responsibil-

.../cont'd

ity for 'portfolios' of business areas. The number of management roles was reduced from 122 to 60, with many roles being undertaken by new teams.

Hand-in-hand with boardroom level and management changes, shopfloor workers were able to ditch the 'them and us' attitude largely aided by the further deployment of teams. These multi-skilled teams of ten workers were responsible for ten work functions, with each team member being capable of four or five functions. Quality levels improved, productivity increased and overall there was a greater awareness of 'the customer' and 'the product'. In this way, the top-down culture of the past was reversed.

Self-managed teams with empowered employees were now at the very core of Baxi and commanded a wide spread of responsibility, but the company also recognised that teams are not intrinsically successful. There have been many problems in overcoming ineffective team functioning. To reflect the emphasis and commitment to the 'new way', training for team members was increased to at least 1% of turnover compared with a previous budget of nil!

The success described above was quite extensively covered in business magazines in the early 1990s. However, the twist to this particular experience is that the CEO who initiated the widespread change initiative left Baxi. A new CEO, with the support of the board, has re-structured some of the business areas affected by the previous changes to alleviate problems experienced with the revised structures. The company now embraces a more evolutionary pace of change and has achieved considerable further success with the deployment of multi-disciplined teams and the use of internal market structures.

At least some of the lessons of the Baxi experience are clear. Be careful in taking at face value all the proclaimed benefits of major changes described in the media. Business transformation almost never runs totally smoothly at the first attempt. Patience and a careful balancing of business change ambition with ongoing key influencer commitment is essential!

Multiskilling

In many respects, multiskilling is the key to successful business process redesign.

Where, in the past, so-called 'specialists' used to do just one element of the job before passing the responsibility on to another 'specialist' who did the next piece of work, one individual now typically tackles several related tasks.

For example, in a traditional sales order processing structure, an order clerk used to record a customer's order before passing the job onto a credit controller to check the customer's credit rating, and then onto a production scheduler to quote a delivery date. In a redesigned work environment, one individual will often carry out these three tasks in rapid sequence, so eliminating the handover delays, errors and confusion of responsibility often associated with the old way of working. In the best new order processing work environments, each customer is handled by just one individual who takes personal responsibility for making sure that the customer is kept fully informed on progress, and that the entire elapsed time between an order being placed and being fulfilled is minimised. The customer is happy, costs are lower and the entire cycle time from enquiry to getting paid is much reduced.

Although there are many examples of successful multiskilling in a wide variety of business environments from manufacturing cells, through supermarkets and motor repair shops, to offices and R&D laboratories, resistance to change is still the norm. While clerical and semi-skilled people have often welcomed moves to greater job responsibility and so-called 'job enrichment', skilled and professional staff have often resisted multiskilling vigorously and with great ingenuity.

The reasons for resisting multiskilling are pretty obvious. First of all, multiskilling does not suit everyone. Individuals who have got used to a fixed routine and a perceived level of status are often reluctant to try something new, particularly where this involves losing their supervisory responsibilities and becoming just one of the multiskilled team workers. Also, some people are just not willing or able to learn a range of new skills very quickly and therefore feel themselves falling behind their colleagues, becoming lost in the new work environment.

The main source of resistance, however, is a perceived change in career path development. Many professional workers have planned their careers along well-worn functional development routes. Trainee accountants aspire one day to become finance directors and bland personnel officers see themselves becoming inspirational human resource directors. Laboratory workers all have their pet theories that will one day be recognised by their peers, leading to publicity, fame, and promotion to chief scientist. All bright young sales and marketing people aspire to become the driving force behind major new product initiatives in just a few years' time. Almost all of these professional workers recognise that achieving their ambitions may require multiple career moves, often involving several different employers.

But almost none of them planned their careers in redesigned work environments. Why on earth should they learn a range of new and often mundane skills that have very little to do with their chosen career path? In the old world they knew that if they could shine as individuals in a particular job or on an important project, then their chances of becoming 'fast track' movers and shakers became much more likely. But now, the emphasis seems to be changing to team performance .... at least in theory. In reality, of course, the old rules still apply and these new-fangled team ideas will blow over in time. Won't they?

Resistance to business process redesign (and the integral ideas of multiskilling and teamwork) by professional workers is likely to remain one of the major obstacles to business transformation for the foreseeable future. The businesses that succeed in overcoming this hurdle will be those that can create new and viable career paths for their core multiskilled employees.

Experience 6: Multiskilling

Western Provident Association

Western Provident Association (WPA) is a private UK health insurance company that enjoyed expansion and consolidation throughout the early '80s, but later faced extinction. They embarked on a reengineering exercise that fashioned customer-oriented IT systems based on two core processes. This enabled workers to handle any type of customer enquiry by working in multi-skilled teams.

In line with these changes was a wholesale de-layering of WPA. The autonomous teams replaced outdated layers of management, and those who opposed the changes (often those with the most to lose from empire demolition) were given the option of redeployment or redundancy. This was one of the most difficult tasks as functional hierarchies have a nasty habit of reinforcing bad practice; and it was hoped that developing teams would not only fundamentally alter formal structures but would also enable those involved to establish a new way of thinking.

However, many did not have a choice: they were told to adopt the new ways or leave. The CEO who initiated the changes deliberately fostered a 'culture of performance' to put pressure on team members and ensure that performance (particularly individual performance as opposed to team performance) was always up to scratch and ever improving. He believed this was the right approach to ensuring that a process-based organisation such as WPA was able to constantly revitalise itself.

The culture of performance is now firmly established at WPA. Process staff are closely scrutinised. Individuals have to fill in detailed performance forms twice daily that describe the length of time they have worked, the number of customer transactions that they have processed, the telephone queries dealt with and the number of customer complaints received.

The system enforces personal accountability to the extreme, so that if any stage of the process breaks down, faults or errors can be traced back to the individuals 'responsible'. It is ironic that WPA's

.../cont'd

attempt at shelving the functional hierarchy actually resulted in a system that in many ways was the antithesis of flexibility, autonomy and teamworking.

Yet this approach has been successful, at least in the short term. Within two years, WPA had been transformed from a loss-making potential insolvent into a market-breaking leader with an impressive array of bottom-line results. Administrative costs were reduced by over 40%, productivity increased 100% and staff turnover was dramatically reduced from 66% to only 8%. In addition, answering customer calls right first time were increased by 80%, the time required to handle new business was reduced from 28 to 4 days, and the time to process a new policy was reduced from 45 to only 4 minutes. Justification, it seems, for their approach to people management and multiskilling.

This is a fascinating experience to evaluate, since it has strong elements of traditional autocracy combined with the delayering and multiskilling principles of modern process redesign. Perhaps the removal of influential blockers to change, combined with the low number of key influencers typically found in routine process jobs, explains the successful management of this major change. As the lessons to be learnt from the WPA experience become clearer over the next few years, it will be interesting to see whether heavy autocracy is really an effective short-term 'shock' to overcome commitment problems, rather than a longer-term business design solution. Watch this space.

Continuous improvement

Continuous improvement is seen by many as the key element of the Japanese quality revolution that had a major impact on world competitiveness during the 1970s and 1980s. As a result, quality circles and other forms of group employee involvement, together with a variety of improvement suggestion schemes have now become commonplace in many Western businesses. One side-effect of this fashion has been the widespread use of quality-related charts scattered on boards in prominent locations around factory and office buildings.

Despite this somewhat frenetic activity, however, only one quality improvement programme in five is now regarded as being a success by those involved. And even in the most successful experiences, relatively modest bottom-line benefits are claimed on an ongoing basis. In a nutshell, the history of continuous improvement over the last two decades can be summarised as follows:

- Those businesses that were amongst the first to significantly improve customer care and achieve a reputation for high-quality products/services were rewarded with a *one-off* gain in market position. Customer care improvements were often achieved by reducing hierarchy and empowering lower-level employees. Product quality improvements were often achieved by replacing traditional quality checks with a 'right first time, every time' philosophy, where each worker corrects any mistakes/defects in a product or service before moving on to complete their own allocated tasks. (Classic examples of this phenomena are the Japanese car manufacturers, whose prodigious growth coincided with this type of one-off competitive leap. As a result, the entire Western car market now competes at a significantly higher quality/customer care level in the 1990s and further competitive gains are much more difficult to achieve.)

- Continuous improvement beyond these types of one-off opportunities have led to only modest measurable benefits. (Partly this is due to competitors continually improving as well, but we believe that the underlying reasons are more profound – see overleaf.)

In our Total Business Design model, we contend that businesses develop in 'spurts', with periods of relative calm between each leap forward. Although the size and frequency of these spurts varies considerably, the pattern is inevitable. Sometimes the spurts are due to new products being developed or new enterprises being created/taken over. On other occasions, the spurts are as a result of major changes in the way that the business machine works, such as when a successful business process redesign is implemented.

In between these spurts, continuous improvement comes into its own – in a modest but quite important way. The primary objective of continuous improvement mechanisms (such as quality groups or

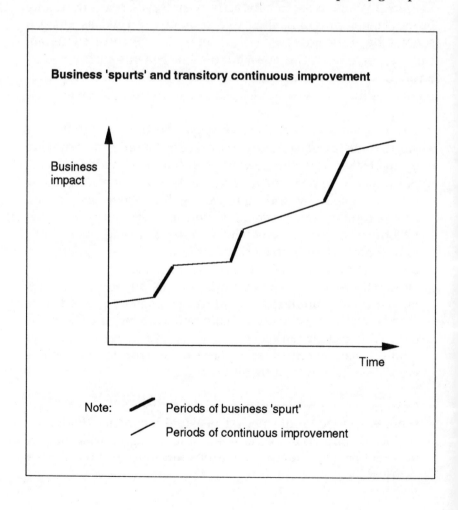

Business 'spurts' and transitory continuous improvement

Business impact

Time

Note: Periods of business 'spurt'

          Periods of continuous improvement

suggestion schemes) is to optimise the processes and activities associated with the current business machine at any point in time. Occasionally, these mechanisms might lead to a further business spurt, although this is relatively rare and more focused mechanisms do exist to identify and exploit major change opportunities.

Before you get either too enthusiastic or too depressed about continuous improvement programmes, consider the following:

• Continuous improvement mechanisms are fine for (usually minor) improvements in the operation of the current business machine.

• These mechanisms work best where an appropriate change/ improvement culture has been successfully established – but this is very difficult to achieve. One precondition for a successful continuous improvement mechanism, for example, is that there should be no fear of redundancies or demotions as a direct result of employee-suggested changes.

• These mechanisms are, by their nature, designed for continual sub-optimisation. The next big business spurt may well replace much of the continuous improvement that has been achieved.

• Continuous improvement eventually withers and dies without external stimulus. Without new ideas on how other organisations are doing things, the law of diminishing returns on the effort put into continuous improvement applies with full vigour.

Strategic alliances:
the power versus the glory

The proportion of value added by Japanese automobile manufacturers is much lower than that of their Western competitors, with the exception of small niche producers. This has nothing to do with productivity. The difference is due to the Japanese practice of purchasing a higher proportion of major finished components from subcontractors, with whom they have a 'strategic alliance'.

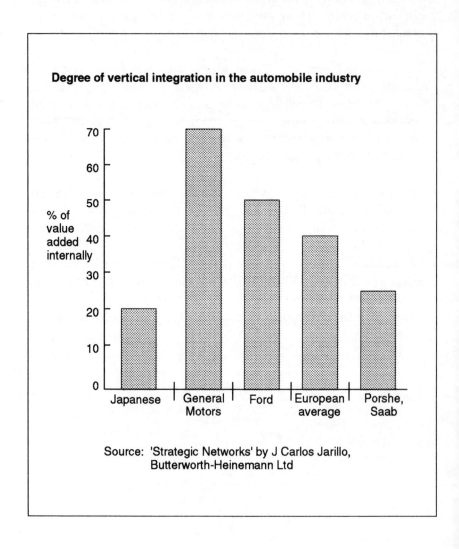

Source: 'Strategic Networks' by J Carlos Jarillo,
Butterworth-Heinemann Ltd

However, if we look at the opposite extreme , we see an historical pattern where highly vertically integrated companies have generally failed to become efficient, low-cost producers. Classic examples of high-cost vertically integrated organisations included General Motors and IBM in the early 1980s .... before commercial pressures forced major change on both these mega-businesses.

In recent years, strategic alliances have become increasingly popular across a whole range of industries, covering activities as diverse as manufacturing, distribution and even the sales process itself. Yet the picture is not universally rosy – far from it. Once again, from a business design perspective, we have a very mixed picture. Once again we need to balance the pros and cons in specific business situations.

In a strategic alliance the purchaser of the products/services is foregoing the right to continually shop around for the best price, in return for a good price and a relationship that guarantees other business benefits. These benefits may, for example, include exclusivity, quality guarantees, timeliness, or a reduction in working costs due to reduced stock levels or reduced administrative costs.

Where strategic alliances are working very effectively, there is usually a recognition of the need for an ongoing 'win-win' relationship by the dominant partner. (The dominant partner in a strategic alliance is often a large business commissioning products or services from a particular large, medium-sized or small supplier.)

Often, successful dominant partners achieve two apparently opposite things at the same time. First, they control the entire value-adding process – from, for example, raw materials through to selling to the final consumer. And control really means control – setting prices, volumes, timescales, levels of quality and even working systems. Second, they do not necessarily *own* the groups that provide them with raw materials or components, nor do they necessarily *own* the groups that commercialise or sell the finished products or services to end customers. In this way, dominant partners act simultaneously as large integrated businesses in a particular market, while actually owning only a fraction of the processes that they control.

However, like many dominant/subservient relationships, things do not always run smoothly. In recent years, one of the most successful companies to exploit strategic alliances has been the clothes retail franchiser, Benetton. Their closely controlled image and marketing activities have dominated their supplier and shop-owner alliances based on, respectively, guaranteed supply volumes and extensive support in advertising, shop layout, uniform pricing and local exclusivity. Yet even Benetton ran into trouble in 1994, as its controversial and sometimes unpopular advertising campaigns (including images of war) led to reduced sales in an already depressed High Street situation. Some shop owners complained bitterly, while a few even withdrew from their agreements in a plethora of legal action. Although many of these problems surfaced in Germany, the fallout reached as far as business TV programmes in the United Kingdom and North America.

An even more dramatic breakdown in strategic alliance relationships occurred when a seemingly harmonious and cooperative alliance between Rover and Honda was shattered by the agreed sale of Rover to BMW. While this relationship seemed to be much more one of equal partners than is the case with Benetton, the Achilles heel turned out to be the motivations of Rover's owners, BAe, rather than the behaviour of the main parties concerned – Rover and Honda.

When evaluating strategic alliances as part of a business design exercise, we believe that ongoing 'win-win' is the key design element. In particular, both parties must address the thorny issue of over-dependency. It is in the medium-term interest of neither party if, for example, a period-end termination of the alliance is synonymous with the bankruptcy of the minor partner. Diversification into other core business areas or into a number of strategic alliances are often real solutions to this problem area. We know of several enlightened dominant partners in strategic alliances who have gone out of their way to provide their minor partners with strategic business advice in this area.

When strategic alliances work well, the result is significantly reduced costs and increased business effectiveness. However, many strategic alliances fail. The power balance in strategic alliances is a key aspect of this increasingly popular business design option. 'Win-win' is not easy to achieve and maintain over time.

Much more frequently, one of the parties achieves an exploitative, dominant position (by chance or design) and the full benefits of the alliance prove elusive.

Experience 7 Strategic alliances

The Telecommunications Industry

The growing trend of strategic alliances forged between companies from different sectors and different continents is epitomised by the telecommunications industry.

There is a quiet revolution taking place under our noses that will have a profound impact on the way we do business in the next millennium. The boundaries between telephone, cable and computer companies are becoming increasingly blurred, as technologies merge together to create very powerful communication tools.

The world's major telecommunications companies are currently constructing a network of strategic alliances that will deliver a potent mix of wireless, computer and cable technologies.

In particular, the benefits that cable and telephone companies can expect to gain from strategic alliances with each other are driving the two industries together. Cable companies have a high capacity for data transmission, but are limited in their ability to offer two-way interactive services. The telephone companies find themselves in the reverse situation: in need of large transmission capacities to exploit their expertise in interactive technologies.

The reasons for alliance are simple enough, but very compelling. For example, Southwestern Bell in the United States requires a cable system to exploit its developments in low power wireless pocket 'phones – linking personal communication devices is not a strength of 'phone systems, but is efficiently carried out via cable. Other examples include 'phone company US West, which has teamed up with AT&T to test a 'movies on demand' system in Colorado. Examples are steadily becoming more common and larger in scale. Future developments will see TVs acting more like 'phones and computers, whilst 'phone lines will carry TV images and computer data. The cable and 'phone companies will continue to compete more directly, but at the same time, cooperate more closely.

.../cont'd

So with the cable and 'phone companies in ever-increasing contact, where does this leave the likes of computer giants such as IBM, Hewlett Packard and Microsoft?

Bill Gates has announced plans for a Microsoft operating system for TVs, with further plans to turn television into a more powerful communications tool in collaboration with Paramount Communications and Time Warner Telecommunications. Apple Computers has entered into an alliance with Sharp, to exploit the Japanese expertise with consumer electronics. In exchange, the Japanese hope to gain from the high-level digital programming skills that American companies are famed for.

The alliances we have described are happening across national boundaries, as well as across industries. In 1993, BT paid $4.3 billion for a 20% stake in MCI Communications, the US long-distance carrier. Between them a further $2 billion will be poured into an initiative that will make the new company one of the few global carriers in the market for global corporate network services. They will not be alone. AT&T, Kokusai Denshin of Japan and Singapore Telecom have already collaborated on a similar project.

As the players in the three (as yet) separate industries come to realise that their future market will be one, the pace at which strategic alliances are made will accelerate.

Benchmarking

Of all the ideas that break the mould, this one most bears a resemblance to the proverbial 'curate's egg'. Where benchmarking is really relevant, it can become a catalyst for massive change. But where comparisons with other businesses are misused, the results can act as aids to the most beleaguered, reactionary and inept managers. The quality of benchmarking data varies hugely – from well-researched, up-to-date and reliable comparisons of similar business processes to superficial semi-guesses.

The following four examples illustrate the range, quality variation and opportunity for abuse of benchmarking:

- City financial analysts provide a form of high-level, strategic benchmarking service based on a combination of financial figures, market analysis and conjecture. A minority of highly competent executives with a clearly thought through business design have been able to overcome gloomy predictions by financial analysts and set course for periods of substantial business growth. A very small minority have achieved similar results by luck. Some particularly inept senior executives have even managed to convert strong market positions to disaster scenarios in remarkably short periods of time (usually by misguided acquisitions or disposals). However, strategic evaluations of this kind have a pretty good track record as a medium-term guide and are usually ignored at your peril (even if they get some of the details wrong). If you are currently faced with adverse financial analysis reports, delay the round of city lunches to improve your PR and make very sure that your total business design has real credibility in the areas that matter.

- In contrast to the routine, strategic financial analysis type of benchmark, there are a growing number of experiences where specific benchmark information on particular aspects of a business's operations are so profound that radical change results. One of the most publicised experiences is that of the Ford motor company in the United States and their purchasing procedures. In the late 1980s, Ford found out that Mazda, in which they had a minority shareholding, spent a small fraction of Ford's overhead on their purchasing and related accounting activities, even after size differences had been taken into consideration. The end result of this piece of information was that Ford radically changed its purchasing procedures for motor parts, stopped matching invoices to delivery notes (an aging sacred cow for accountants) and reduced relevant staff numbers by some 75%. (By the way, the authors of this book look forward to the day when the ultimate sacred cow of the accounting profession – the double entry recording system – is slaughtered by a major business. When you hear of this happening, let us know.)

• One of the most widely used, and ineffective, benchmarks is that for IT systems development productivity. This is partly due to the imprecise nature of the measurements available in a rapidly changing systems development environment. But mostly the ineffectiveness of these measures is due to the motivation for obtaining this often spurious information in the first place. A few years ago, one conglomerate had a corporate IT service that's reputation was exceptionally poor amongst IT users. The IT Director, however, rebuffed all criticism with the statement that "we run a very efficient IT shop – our systems productivity is in the 'upper quartile' on two separate independent benchmarks". Not surprisingly, this IT shop was eventually outsourced when the user community came to the conclusion that they were tired of having poor systems developed very efficiently. In contrast, a major insurance company with an above average central IT service also had benchmark ratings in the 'upper quartile' for systems development productivity. Rather than celebrating, they changed their system development approach quite radically and succeeded in doubling their measured productivity over a two-year period .... and as we write, they are still in the 'upper quartile' of the benchmark! They have not been outsourced.

• One large chemicals company decided to initiate an internal benchmarking exercise to compare methods and productivities achieved in some of its fundamental administrative processes (such as order processing, credit control and accounts administration). Since one team was responsible for establishing the mechanism and gathering/evaluating the measurements taken, the end results were very accurate. Over a period of three years, their administrative productivity across all the main divisions had risen to a uniformly high level. In some of the most striking examples, productivity and cycle time improvements of more than 50% were achieved.

The lessons of benchmarking are therefore very clear. Measure only what is really important and never be satisfied with the results.

'Small is beautiful'

In his book 'Global Paradox', John Naisbitt (the 'Megatrends' man) publicised a significant business design trend that came very much into fashion in the late 1980s. The reaction to large, bureaucratic, slow and inflexible organisations spawned 'smallness' as a solution, as well as business process reengineering and a variety of other related ideas.

Almost by stealth, small businesses have come to dominate the big Western economies. For example, only seven per cent of United States exports are now created by companies with 500 or more employees. The Fortune 500 now accounts for only ten per cent of the American economy, compared with 20 per cent in 1970. And no less than 50 per cent of United States exports are created by businesses with fewer than 20 employees. Similar trends are occurring in other major Western economies, including the United Kingdom.

Many big companies now recognise that they have to dismantle bureaucracy to survive. Economies of scale are giving way to economies of scope, finding the right (typically small) size of organisation for synergy, market flexibility and, above all, speed. For example, ABB (Asea Brown Boveri) one of the world's largest power engineering groups with revenues of more than $30 billion, is organised into 1,200 different companies. Each company employs on average only some 200 people. And its head office has been reduced from 4,000 staff to fewer than 200. Similarly, in 1993, IBM UK's sales operation was divided into 30 separate businesses, each of which on its own authority can fix prices and costs and be totally responsible to its customers. Headquarters staff were reduced from over 2,000 to less than 100 people.

Other large companies following this trend include AT&T, Alcoa, Ciba, General Electric, Grand Metropolitan, Coca-Cola, Johnson & Johnson, BP, Honda, Spring Ram and Xerox.

Another area in which the 'small is beautiful' maxim is being applied is in local (and central) government in the UK. By introducing the concept of customers/service providers for internal services, combined with extensive outsourcing of non-core services, the size of each semi-autonomous unit is radically reduced. In central government, this phenomenon has taken the form of separating policy units from service providers, most of whom are now organised into semi-autonomous government agencies.

In applying the small is beautiful design criteria to a Total Business Design exercise, the key decision is not one of principle – we believe that monolithic organisations are *always* bureaucratic and inefficient. The key design skill is in determining the optimal boundaries for the various business units.

If you make the design too fine (very small business units, for example), then synergy may be missed and additional overheads may result. If you make the design too coarse (with large business units) bureaucracy tends to persist and flexibility/speed of response suffers. The key to success is in the logic of the business boundaries and in getting the design balance right. There are always pros and cons related to each design decision. Clear solutions that are indisputable are rare. Other aspects of business design come into the picture. Realistic design options come at different levels. And the 'knee jerk' reaction of arbitrarily limiting the maximum size of business units to (say) 200 or 300 people is almost always wrong.

We find that the viability of this type of business design can be thoroughly tested by considering the likely new working environment and potential problems in a design simulation workshop and by incorporation into a Total Business Design viability test (described later). In the simulation workshops, debate around the key business objectives in relation to the realistic design options is often more productive than working through checklists of theoretical design rules.

'Smallness' is yet another good business design concept. It is also a fashion, and not a panacea.

Experience 8: Small is beautiful

AT&T

In many ways, AT&T typified the large, cumbersome bureaucracies that flourished up until the mid-1980s. Driven by 'economies of scale' and notions of 'efficiency through size', these companies often gorged on national economies, becoming bloated and slower in their response to the market.

In 1984, the US government split the sprawling AT&T monopoly into seven regional companies (the 'Baby Bells'), leaving 'Ma Bell' with the long-distance business. Since then, AT&T has shed some 140,000 jobs, ceded 30 per cent of the long-distance market to competitors and struggled to develop its computer business.

But the AT&T story also has some notable successes. The launch of the Universal Card made AT&T the second biggest credit card issuer in the United States, and helped increase the loyalty of long-distance customers. The acquisition of McCaw Cellular Communications in 1994 was a smart move to gain a strong position in the wireless communications market. And, in recent years, customers have benefited from lower long-distance call charges and an array of new services.

Now AT&T is breaking up again in a bold move to capitalise on the forthcoming deregulation of the telecommunications industry, which will allow long-distance suppliers into local markets – and the Baby Bells will be able to offer long-distance services. AT&T is embarking on the biggest voluntary corporate break-up in history, devolving itself into three publicly traded entities covering long-distance and credit-card businesses, telecommunications equipment manufacturing, and computers.

Interestingly, this perseverance along the 'small is beautiful' path is in stark contrast to the merger mania that is rife in the media/ entertainment world, pharmaceuticals and banking. The AT&T demerger, however, has been welcomed on Wall Street, where financial analysts' initial reactions have been positive. They believe that the slimmed-down giant will become a formidable competitor for the Baby Bells as deregulation progresses.

'Information age' products and services

Leading academics and gurus (such as Stan Davis, formerly of the Harvard Business School and now a leading consultant) are predicting that we are currently seeing the end of the industrial age and have already started to live in the 'information age' .... and even the beginnings of the 'knowledge age'.

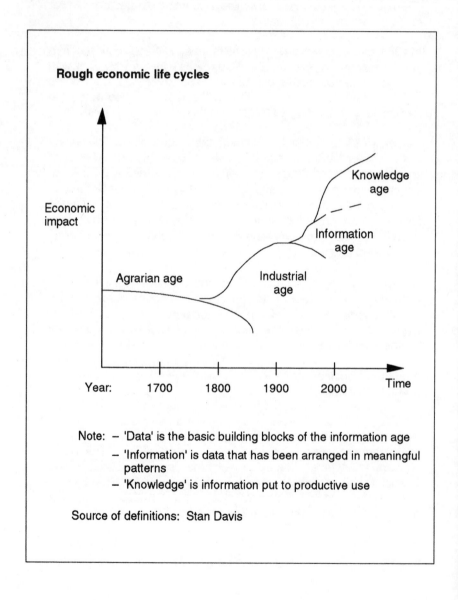

Rough economic life cycles

Economic impact

Knowledge age

Information age

Agrarian age

Industrial age

Year: 1700   1800   1900   2000   Time

Note: – 'Data' is the basic building blocks of the information age
       – 'Information' is data that has been arranged in meaningful patterns
       – 'Knowledge' is information put to productive use

Source of definitions: Stan Davis

Already we can track the increasingly important part that information is playing in the process of adding value to products. 'Smarter' physical products are more-and-more being seen as key strategic moves to provide differentiation advantages against low-cost commodity products from the Pacific Basin and elsewhere. Leading examples of 'information rich' physical products include:

- Smart car tyres, which contain a microchip that collects and analyses data about air pressure. Goodyear and others are working on this type of product, which eventually will be able to flash a message to the car dashboard that says "Low tyre pressure – time for a pit stop".

- Smart glass has been developed (by an American company, Suntec) that can either reflect or transmit 90% of the sun's rays, depending on the internal temperature. When the internal temperature of a car or office, for example, reaches 71 degrees, the glass starts to reflect radiant heat back into the atmosphere.

Service products are also getting 'smarter' as businesses strive for competitive advantage through increased innovation. Typical examples of this approach include:

- The Ritz-Carlton hotel chain, which has installed a knowledge-based computer system to keep track of customer preferences and needs (such as smoking habits and special dietary requirements) and to communicate this information worldwide. Even very specialised preferences, such as hypoallergenic pillows, can be catered for automatically to improve customer service .... and competitiveness.

- The Citibank Advantage system that can identify unusual credit card transactions and initiate action to check with customers that no fraud has taken place. This system is expected to get smarter and smarter as it learns from each customers' patterns of routine (and even non-routine) activity over time.

Another interesting aspect of the information age is the increasing number of businesses where secondary information-based services have become important contributors to the bottom line .... and in some cases now dominate traditional business activities. Well-known examples of this phenomenon include:

- The computer-generated airline guides and reservation systems, such as American Airline's SABRE system, which in recent years has been much more profitable than the airline business itself.

- One of the best-selling magazines in most Western countries is the leading magazine covering TV schedules for the coming week – for example, the 'Radio Times' in the United Kingdom. In many countries, this publication represents a business that is as profitable as the respective TV programme commissioning and transmission business. (Interestingly, these publications are likely to come under considerable competitive pressure as smart electronic alternatives are developed to help viewers scan and select from the content of literally dozens of new TV channels as we move into the new millennium.)

Viewed from a Total Business Design perspective, however, these new developments are just additional inputs to the learning organisation model and the core business concepts model.

By selecting the relevant new age products that apply to your own business environment and running these through the Kay model of core business, issues such as the likely impact on existing products, new product opportunities, and timeframes for action can all be objectively assessed.

The learning organisation model can be used to cross-check that suitable information channels are in place, so that new developments (from both inside and outside your particular business environment) can be effectively monitored and evaluated. In extreme cases, where the future of current core business is seriously under threat, the radical remedies suggested by the learning organisation model may provide a 'life-raft' to a new business world .... at a price.

Stealing manufacturing ideas

Many of the ideas that now break the mould in office environments started life as manufacturing techniques. One of the first manifestations of 'empowerment', for example, was in cellular manufacturing and in the 'right first time, every time' approach to quality developed by Japanese manufacturers. 'Just In time' (JIT) techniques used in many manufacturing and purchasing processes form the basis of much business process redesign thinking – particularly the redesign elements that seek to squeeze time out of business processes.

Similarly, the traditional relationships between manufacturers and dominant retailers (such as big clothing retailers and supermarkets) form the basis of much strategic supplier thinking in business design today

We believe that those techniques obviously 'stolen' from manufacturing so far for use in other environments are really just the tip of the iceberg. Many large information-based businesses bear a close relationship to manufacturing processes. For example, subsets of the very sophisticated scheduling techniques developed for use in factory environments have obvious application in high-volume information processes, such as insurance policy generation and claims administration.

Also, the principles of Perpetual Inventory (an auditing technique developed to progressively refine those sub-systems that support key data accuracy within a Manufacturing Resources Planning (MRP) environment) have found a new use in the ongoing maintenance of market research/demographic data. The technique involves auditing key data by reference to its relative importance to the overall system. This, in its original manufacturing guise, encourages ever increasing levels of accuracy in bills-of-material, process routeings and inventory balances. A major consequence of using this approach is the eventual demise of the all-embracing periodic stock-take which, historically, has simply generated a new set of incorrect numbers. In its new, innovative form, perpetual inventory techniques are obviating regular, large-scale censuses in favour of continual, little-but-often, reviews of the key data-sets, and the progressive refinement of relevant support systems.

We expect a steady 'drip feed' of new ideas that break the mould coming from revised manufacturing techniques for at least the next five years. For those adopting the Total Business Design approach, these new techniques can be clinically reviewed in terms of importance to the business, and selectively used to revise the business design. In contrast, those who continue to work in blissful ignorance of the Total Business Design approach will carry on riding the new business idea 'fashion' rollercoaster for a rough ride through high expectations, disillusion and then partial enlightenment.

Coaches, not leaders?

The public's perception of business leaders has fluctuated over the last 50 years and continues to do so. High-profile figures, such as the visionary Bill Gates of Microsoft, the hard-hitting Lord King of British Airways, the charismatic Richard Branson of Virgin, the softly spoken Lord Weinstock of GEC, the jovial John Harvey Jones, and the transatlantic Hanson/White duo have provided very different types of role model in recent times.

During the 1980s there was considerable speculation that the macho manager would make a comeback in the vacuum provided by the rapid decline in trade union influence and power in the United Kingdom. Somewhat surprisingly, however, the opposite seems to be the case. Modern concepts of delayering and empowerment have led to the idea of the 'coaching' manager. The essential differences between coaching and old-style delegation of responsibility are summarised below.

Comparison of delegation and performance coaching

Delegation	Coaching
1. Delegate to get work done.	Delegate to develop the individual.
2. Do not delegate decision making.	Delegate decisions of low impact initially. Gradually delegate more important decisions.
3. Avoid risks.	Accept that there are risks in delegation.
4. Criticise mistakes.	Accept some mistakes are inevitable. Use these as a learning process.
5. Do not waste time discussing completed tasks.	Take time to discuss the outcome of delegated tasks.

The impetus towards coaching managers was driven by the practical realities of delayered organisational structures. When the middle managers and supervisors had gone, there was an overwhelming need to delegate responsibility to some individual or some team. Although (in the best examples) this approach has led to much greater job satisfaction by those now empowered, the primary rationale was almost always to push authority closer to the interface with the customer .... and to cope with day-to-day work in the absence of delayered workers.

In practice, we have found that the coaching required by any one individual is not consistent, but changes over time at different rates with different people. Although many academics and consultants have put forward frameworks for coaching requirements, we have found the approach developed by Paul Hersey and Kenneth Blanchard in the United States both easy to understand and practical to use.

Hersey and Blanchard believe that the relationship between manager and subordinate moves through a four-phase life cycle as subordinates develop and mature, and that managers need to change their management style with each phase.

In the first phase, an inexperienced subordinate needs to be familiarised with the work environment and relevant roles/tasks that need to be undertaken. In this phase therefore the management style should be highly directive – "do this, do that, don't do that, etc" – with almost no scope for delegation of decision making or participative interaction.

In phase two, as subordinates begin to understand the work environment, a directive style of management remains partially necessary but increasingly responsibility can be delegated and a coaching management style becomes appropriate.

In the third phase, subordinates actively seek greater responsibility and the manager no longer needs to be directive. At this point, a supportive leadership style is needed. As subordinates become increasingly self-reliant, the level of support required (such as help with unusual or complex tasks) is gradually reduced.

By the fourth phase, subordinates are fully prepared to act on their own initiative and complete delegation becomes possible in appropriate areas of activity. Subordinates no longer need or expect a directive relationship with their manager. (Of course, not all subordinates will make it through to phase four.)

As organisations change to accommodate the results of downsizing and delayering, more responsibility is falling onto teams as well as

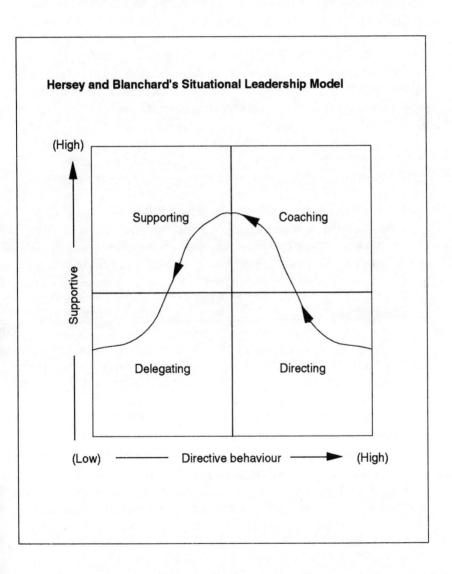

Hersey and Blanchard's Situational Leadership Model

onto individuals. In creating effective business designs for teams with devolved responsibilities, we therefore also need to look at leadership issues in teams.

Fortunately, we can select from a wealth of material developed by historical research into teamworking to assist in this design process. While we remain unconvinced by much of the popular enthusiasm for physically based teambuilding exercises, a minority of the psychometric profiling techniques available have proved useful. In particular, the work of Professor Meredith Belbin and his associates into possible team roles is easy to use in real work situations. The Belbin approach is also unusual in being easy to understand and administer, and thereby minimises the antagonism and fear often associated with psychometric testing. Terms used, such as shaper and plant, even incorporate an element of fun.

The key concept behind the Belbin approach can be summarised by a memorable quote from Belbin himself, describing the results of a multi-team workshop exercise in solving business problems:

> "In human affairs nothing should be taken for granted. That a team of the cleverest people should win in an exercise that placed a premium on cleverness seemed fairly obvious. Such an elementary principle was at least worth checking before any more subtle variations in team design were made. It was as well that we did. The team with the cleverest members finished last."

The discovery that an effective team was not necessarily one composed of the brightest individuals (or even those with just the best skill mix for the task) led Belbin and his colleagues to identify the different team 'roles' that people adopt when working in teams. As well as identifying nine specific team roles, the Belbin work eventually led to rules on the best combinations of role types to mix into a team to achieve an effective result .... both in terms of team cohesiveness, and effectiveness in getting the job done on time. Combined with an appropriate mix of business skills and knowledge, the Belbin role types can be used to maximise the chances of excellent team performance. The nine Belbin team role types are outlined opposite.

The nine Belbin team roles

Team-role contribution	Allowable weaknesses
Co-ordinator: Mature, confident, a good chairperson. Clarifies goals, promotes decision-making, delegates well. A good team leader.	Can be seen as manipulative. Delegates personal work.
Shaper: Challenging, dynamic, thrives on pressure. Has the drive and courage to overcome obstacles. Good in crises. A rapid decision maker.	Can provoke others. Hurts people's feelings.
Plant: Creative, imaginative, unorthodox. Solves difficult problems.	Ignores details. Too preoccupied to communicate effectively.
Resource investigator: Extrovert, enthusiastic, communicative. Explores opportunities. Develops contacts.	Overoptimistic. Loses interest once initial enthusiasm has passed.
Monitor evaluator: Sober, strategic and discerning. Sees all options. Judges accurately.	Lacks drive and ability to inspire others. Overly critical.
Teamworker: Cooperative, mild, perceptive and diplomatic. Listens, builds, averts friction, calms the waters.	Indecisive in crunch situations. Can be easily influenced.

Modified from "Team Roles at Work" by Meredith Belbin, Butterworth-Heinemann Ltd

.../cont'd

The nine Belbin team roles (continued)

Team-role contribution	Allowable weaknesses
Implementer: Disciplined, reliable, conservative and efficient. Turns ideas into practical actions.	Somewhat inflexible. Slow to respond to new possibilities.
Completer: Painstaking, conscientious, anxious. Searches out errors and omissions. Delivers on time.	Inclined to worry unduly. Reluctant to delegate. Can be a nit-picker.
Specialist: Single-minded, self-starting, dedicated. Provides knowledge and skills in rare supply.	Contributes on only a narrow front. Dwells on technicalities. Overlooks the 'big picture'.

Modified from "Team Roles at Work" by Meredith Belbin, Butterworth-Heinemann Ltd

One of the important indicators from a Belbin analysis of team roles (which can be determined by carrying out relevant discussions and a twenty-minute individual questionnaire) is the most appropriate characteristics for team leaders.

Indeed, by extending the Belbin indicators to make allowances for the type of work to be carried out, it is possible to identify the different team leaders who are likely to perform best in different work situations – such as in periods of radical change or in periods of continuous steady improvement with well-established colleagues. By using a suitable combination of skill/knowledge requirements, personal judgements and Belbin team leadership attributes as part of personal competencies, the choice of leader for different work environments is increasingly becoming a science, rather than the Black Art of old. This capability is one of the key ingredients in a practical learning organisation as executives' understanding of Total Business Design matures.

In the area of business leadership, one trend is clear and ongoing. The business leaders of tomorrow will be much better educated in the realities of change management than those of today. A new cadre of business executives is emerging and they will progressively inherit the positions of power. In future, charisma will be much less important than a good understanding of practical business design.

~ 7 ~
Implementing major change effectively

Earlier we described the four big hurdles to effective, major change in large and medium-sized organisations – lack of commitment, piecemeal fashion-driven approaches, ineffective change training and lethargic IT systems. These are indeed the most serious obstacles to implementing a successful major change programme, and more than 80% of businesses fail to overcome them.

However, a small minority of businesses have overcome these hurdles and have moved on to encounter new and different problems. These next-level problems typically include:

• Inadequate implementation mechanisms.

• Project management and phasing imbalances.

• Inadequate, and often contradictory, use of the available channels of communication.

• Mixed and patchy motivational levels.

In this section, we make recommendations on change techniques to overcome both the high-level, big hurdles to business transformation and these lower-level problems.

Getting effective commitment:
the 'Influencer Balance Analysis' approach

Our research has shown conclusively that, with the exception of acquisitions/disposals, high-level structural change and change in people numbers, it is insufficient for *just* senior executives to be committed to a major change initiative. Large numbers of organisations have failed to achieve change with only this type of top-level support.

What is also required for successful major change in the business machine is commitment from a number of other key influencers. It is often difficult to identify these influencers because they do not reside at obvious levels of management. Key influencers can be

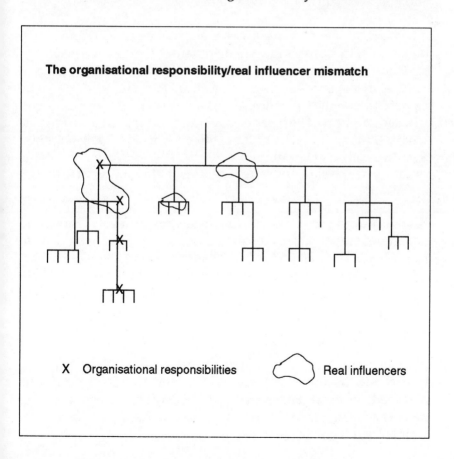

The organisational responsibility/real influencer mismatch

X Organisational responsibilities   Real influencers located in several levels of the organisation, although the majority will typically reside near the top. When senior executives attempt to identify key influencers at lower levels, they typically get at least one-third of the people wrong.

In developing the Total Business Design approach, we therefore needed a mechanism to identify the potential for achieving a critical balance of support amongst those key individuals who can implement, or block, change in the business machine.

The approach we developed is called Influencer Balance Analysis (IBA). This specific measure can accurately gauge the likelihood of success in a major change exercise very early on. In addition, if success seems initially unlikely, it can clearly indicate the individuals who will need convincing .... or replacing.

In a situation where a major change initiative is *not* about to be undertaken, IBA can gauge whether there is a ground swell of key influencers who actually advocate change. It works both ways – either a major change programme has or hasn't got adequate support among the influencers, or the status quo has or hasn't got sufficient support. The ideal position for an innovative business is to have a preponderance of innovative forces for change at both executive and other key influencer levels. We believe that IBA-type commitment measures are a key ingredient of a successful learning organisation.

IBA is a two-stage process that first measures the level of influence that an individual has (by asking others) and the degree to which that individual is in favour of, or against, a specified major change initiative. Secondly, IBA provides insights into the support balances for each significant aspect of the proposed change, so that very unpopular elements of a large change programme can be critically reviewed.

Interviews are normally started at executive level and spread throughout the other influencers. As the key influencers are identified, the same names are mentioned again and again during the interviewing process. When new names cease to be mentioned, the interviewing process stops.

Typical pattern for identifying key influencers

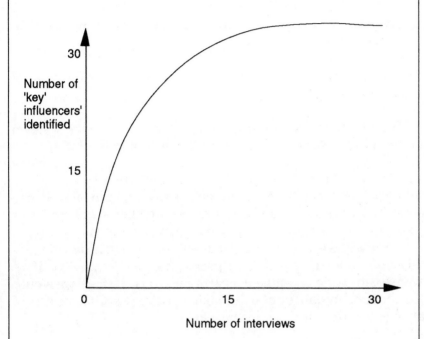

Number of
'key'
influencers'
identified

30

15

0   15   30

Number of interviews

Note: For a major change initiative covering large areas of the business, we typically find that there are about 30 'key influencers', including a high proportion of top executives.

Note: Typically between 10 and 15 interviews are necessary to identify all the 'key influencers'.

We have deliberately chosen interviews, as opposed to question-naires, since these provide a more comprehensive way of gathering sensitive information. Interviewees are asked four main questions:

1. The names of the people whom they regard as being key influencers.

2. The relative position of the identified individuals in relation to each other, in terms of influence.

3. The influence of these individuals in terms of specific areas of change.

4. The rough position of these individuals on a change scale: in favour of a particular change initiative, or not.

In summary, these interviews identify the patterns for the weight of influence and the individual's rough position on a pro/anti change scale. In this way, we can rapidly assess whether or not sufficient balance of support exists for a major change initiative. However, these measures give a picture of overall support and do not identify levels of support for particular aspects of the change initiative. If we were to stop the commitment measurement at this stage, we would therefore be in danger of overlooking critical, specific aspects of change that have little or no support.

The next stage, typically, is therefore to set up three- or four-day workshops for executives and for the other identified key influencers. The first day entails selective education for all those participating to ensure a reasonably consistent level of understanding of change ideas and experiences. The final two or three days build a vision of what the 'new world' will look like at a fairly detailed level. The balance of support for each aspect of the change proposed is then measured and recorded on appropriately designed questionnaires – for later, more detailed, analysis.

The deliverables from the two-stage IBA process are therefore:

• An initial assessment of support for an overall major change initiative. If the balance in favour of the proposed changes is poor, then the initiative needs to be reviewed urgently – either the proposed changes are flawed or we need to change some of the key players in the game.

* A refined assessment of support balances for specific aspects of the proposed change initiative. Again, if the support for specific areas of change is poor, then these areas need to be reviewed. In practice, we find that the workshop 'vision' debates often produce very constructive revisions to initial change proposals – for the simple reason that these workshops only take place once an overall positive change balance has been achieved for the initiative as a whole.

By adopting the IBA approach, you can identify the good and bad news very early in a major change process. The resulting savings in money, disruption, time, energy and credibility can be massive.

Influencer balance analysis: concepts and 'mechanics'

Area of influence: Sales processes

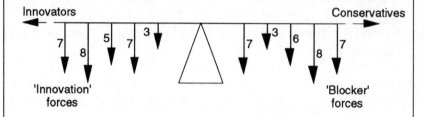

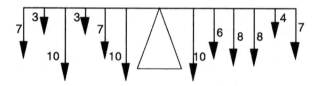

Note: Balance forces are calculated as follows for each area of influence:

Sum of: 'Influencer rating' x 'Innovator rating' for all relevant individuals

compared with

Sum of: 'Influencer rating' x 'Conservative rating' for all relevant individuals

Note: Both 'influencer' ratings and 'innovator/conservative' ratings are assessed on a 1–10 scale.

Experience 9: Getting effective commitment – The Leicester Royal Infirmary

One of the select few early successes of National Health Service reform in the United Kingdom was a radical process redesign exercise carried out at the Leicester Royal Infirmary NHS Trust. Leicester Royal Infirmary is one of the country's largest teaching hospitals with over 4,000 staff and annual revenues in excess of £100 million.

Outpatient services provide some 15% of the Trust's income and it was this area of operation that led a series of changes at the hospital.

Until 1992 the outpatient processes were typical of traditional units of this type. For example, the neurology outpatient consultation process took between six and 12 weeks, with patients typically visiting the hospital three, four or even five times for a range of specialist tests carried out by different departments, spread round the hospital. Visits to each department had to be coordinated with up-to-date patient notes – some 20 % of which were normally missing or incomplete. Each new outpatient generated 70 minutes of administrative activity and for each subsequent visit a further 30 minutes of administrative work was added. In many respects this process typified old-fashioned hospital bureaucracy.

In the autumn of 1992, however, the hospital began an experiment with its one-stop, one-day, single-visit clinic. This involved the redesign of the outpatient process based on the requirements of individual patients and was modelled on the American Mayo Clinic, where the rich and famous are treated as very valued customers. In the new outpatient process, tests are carried out to meet the needs of patients during one visit, rather than patients arriving to fit in with capacity schedules for testing equipment and specialist resources in different departments. The full service one-stop clinic was introduced in January 1993, with impressive results:

- A 65% reduction in service delivery times.

- A 90% reduction in error rates.

.../cont'd

- A 70% reduction in overall costs.

But why should this exercise have succeeded when many others failed, or just didn't to get off the ground at all? Seven key factors made the difference at Leicester:

- Initial impetus provided by a government grant.

- Clear and measurable objectives.

- Strong commitment by the hospital Chief Executive, Peter Homa.

- Strong commitment by a consultant neurologist (and, we believe, key influencer) Dr Millac.

- A multifunctional project team, led by a senior health service quality specialist seconded for four days a week for a six-month period (another indication of commitment).

- An extensive internal marketing campaign across all relevant departments.

- The appointment of a single person to organise the outpatients journey along the revised process chain.

We believe that this exceptional achievement was founded on a positive senior executive and other key influencer balances in favour of the radical changes. The other factors listed above, although beneficial, often also exist in failed projects.

The 'shadow' organisation of influencers

Business research over the years has frequently highlighted a fundamental difference between formal organisation structures and informal work relationships.

While much of this research has been fragmented and of dubious value, we have been able to draw on one powerful theme that has permeated many such efforts. We describe this theme as 'the shadow organisation': an organisation separate and very different from the organisation chart, which consists of influencers of different types in a variety of jobs.

The fundamental difference between a formal organisation and a shadow organisation of influencers is that:

• The formal organisation determines the overwhelming majority of day-to-day activities and operational decisions. The formal organisation holds sway right across all routine aspects of the business, from factory floor operatives and accounts clerks, through to R&D technicians and sales staff.

• The shadow organisation largely determines change in the business. Where the shadow and formal organisations come into conflict in a change situation, the balance of influence in the shadow organisation will almost always win the day .... or force an exhausting and indeterminate draw.

Clearly the shadow organisation will be segmented amongst the three main types of influencer that we discussed earlier:

• Executive influencers, where a positive balance of individuals can drive successful high-level change.

• Other key influencers at lower organisational levels, who can support or block proposed changes in the business machine.

• Local influencers, who have much less power than either of the above types of influencers, but who can nevertheless speed up or slow down detailed changes at a local level.

For a 1,000-person business, there are likely to be up to ten or 12 executive influencers, up to 30 or 40 other key influencers, and up to 100 local influencers.

By using Influencer Balance Analysis techniques, we are now in a unique position. We can objectively analyse and measure the shadow organisation for the first time. By identifying these different influencer types by individual, we can manage change through the shadow organisation. No longer need we rely on individual executive's views and prejudices.

We believe that the ability to manage all types of change through regular measurement of the shadow organisation represents a fundamental breakthrough in the science of change management. More than any other insight in the Total Business Design approach, the measured shadow organisation of influencers will change the way that enlightened executives run businesses.

We believe that the measured shadow organisation approach will profoundly change the way that a whole raft of fashionable techniques will be applied .... from BPR and TQM through to large IT projects and the practice of learning organisations.

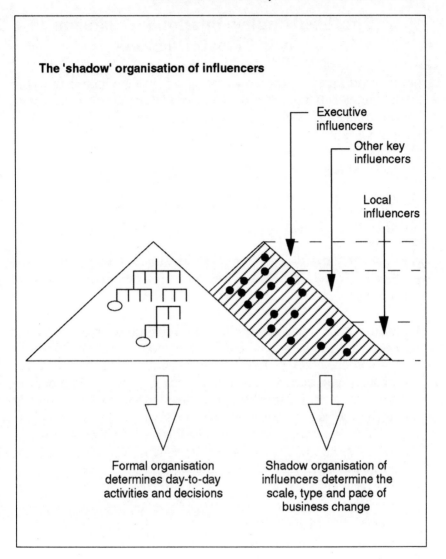

The 'shadow' organisation of influencers

Executive influencers

Other key influencers

Local influencers

Formal organisation determines day-to-day activities and decisions

Shadow organisation of influencers determine the scale, type and pace of business change

The 'best' implementation mechanism .... using key influencers

Before reading these pages on the 'best' implementation mechanism for major change, please bear in mind that there is no universal best approach for all change programmes and all businesses. Also remember that standard change methods are meant for the blind obedience of the legions of 'so-so' consultants .... and for the guidance of wise executives.

The unique change management elements of the Total Business Design approach are based on three simple principles:

- Major change to the business machine should only be attempted when all the relevant senior executives and other key influencers understand the proposed changes and their full implications.

- No such major change should be initiated unless there is a clear *balance* of both senior executives and other key influencers in favour of the change. In other words, both groups should have a positive balance, not just the senior executives. Also bear in mind that a minority of sceptical influencers can be useful in controlling excessive zeal: a total massacre of the non-believers can therefore often be counter-productive. This principle also applies for significant areas of change within a larger business change initiative.

- Key influencers who are strongly in favour of the proposed changes should be seconded to lead both the detailed design phase and the implementation phase of the change programme. Ideally this secondment should be full time, although a heavy part-time commitment may sometimes be sufficient.

By using the Influencer Balance Analysis approach described earlier, we are in a strong position to prepare a change implementation plan where all the main elements of change are supported by a positive balance of both senior executives and key influencers. Where necessary, new innovative people have been introduced to positions of influence and some individuals opposed to the proposed changes have been removed. In this way the odds on success are stacked in our favour from the beginning. We can now begin implementation.

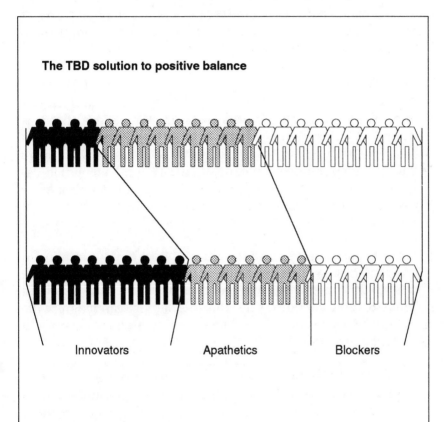

The TBD solution to positive balance

Innovators   Apathetics   Blockers

Note: The objective of an Influencer Balance Analysis exercise is to provide the essential measurements of influencer balances for a change initiative. Once these measurements are available, and before the implementation process starts, it is essential to achieve a positive balance of influencers in the area concerned .... by bringing in 'new blood', removing blockers and convincing the apathetics.

During a major change programme, there is usually a range of activities that need to be carried out both serially and in parallel. Small task forces, coordinated by a central team of executives and influencers, have proved very effective in this type of environment. The central coordinating team typically also maintains a knowledge base of change activities supporting the evolving change implementation plan. Using the change implementation plan as a basis, the initial tasks in the detailed change design and implementation processes are therefore:

• To decide on the pace of change. Should it be a series of 'big bang' changes in rapid succession or should progress be more cautious and 'trickle' through the organisation? We believe that it is essential that the high-level change implementation plan should clearly identify the big bang changes for which there is a positive balance of commitment before significant implementation begins. This helps to ensure that one change does not hamper another and that change elements can be carried out in a logical sequence.

If this is not done, you run the risk of delays or poor training in one change area having a knock-on effect on other changes. We refer to this phenomenon as the 'change interference' effect. In some extreme circumstances, this interference can magnify the early declines in productivity/effectiveness often associated with a change process.

As a rule of thumb, we believe that major change should be implemented in meaningful, quite big elements, rather than in cautious bits and pieces. This level of ambition is only realistic where positive commitment balances exist and where interference effects can be avoided. Most failures in attempting big bang change implementation have been due to poor commitment balances.

• To identify and agree on the individuals who will lead the change design and implementation task forces. These individuals should be chosen from the high-weighted innovators identified during the interview and workshop processes of the Influencer Balance Analysis. For important change initiatives, task-force leaders

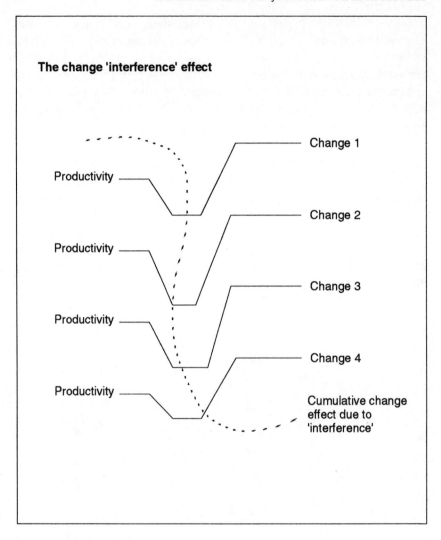

The change 'interference' effect

should be seconded full-time until the key changes are implemented.

These task-force leaders should then choose the people they need in their respective teams, based on their own assessment of the skills, personalities and innovative qualities needed for success. Typically, for important changes, a core of individuals will be seconded to each task force full-time, with others working on a part-time basis as their particular skills are needed.

However, in choosing the core members of each task force, we need to ensure that one or two individuals are also members (or at least observers) of other task forces. This needs to be carefully designed up-front to ensure that a coherent and consistent change vision is maintained across all the task-force activities, and that ideas/ solutions identified in one task force are effectively communicated to all the task forces for selective use and enhancement.

Once a relevant task force is established, we embark on a structured process of workshops and design/implementation tasks. Once again, we use the workshop format because of its benefits in terms

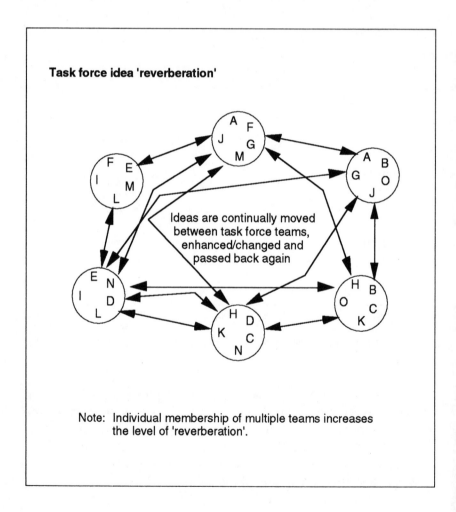

Task force idea 'reverberation'

Ideas are continually moved between task force teams, enhanced/changed and passed back again

Note: Individual membership of multiple teams increases the level of 'reverberation'.

Design and implementation processes

Start point: Each task force leader is a Key Influencer and positive innovator, suitably educated – the remaining task force members are somewhat 'uneducated' at the beginning.

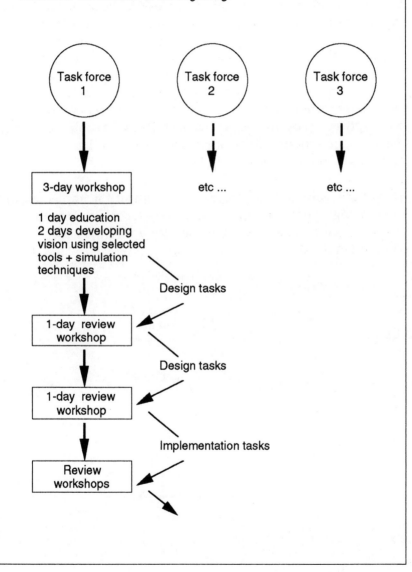

of communicating a consistent vision of the desired environment to all concerned, and because of the need repeatedly to simulate new designs and implementation processes. In effect, we are also using these workshops to replace traditional progress meetings, with specific tasks being carried out by individuals or small sub-taskforces between workshop events.

As design work moves into implementation, the same workshop simulation approach is used progressively at lower levels. The approach that was first used for design is next used for implementation phasing, and finally used as part of user education .... both pre- and post- implementation. In this way, the critical soft training elements are tackled effectively. The number of workshops and task iterations will vary considerably, depending on the size, depth and scope of the proposed changes. In some cases, only one or two iterations will be necessary, while in others numerous iterations over many months will be needed.

When you evaluate this powerful mechanism for implementing major change, bear in mind that it can be used to force through ill-advised changes, as well as highly desirable ones. The mechanism is not judgmental.

Channels of communication
.... using key influencers

One of the lower-profile elements of any major change exercise that must be carried out proficiently is communicating the right messages to the workforce, at the right time.

Alas, this aspect of change is rarely handled well and is often tackled as an afterthought. In the absence of a clear and consistent message, the rumour mill moves into overdrive. Those confidential minutes somehow get partially photocopied and misinterpreted. And, even when the secretaries are highly professional in maintaining confidentiality, there are always one or two senior executives who feel that it is OK to inform a few proteges of what is really going on .... 'off the record'. The rumour mill builds and builds. Naive assumptions about security of sensitive information lead directly to uncertainty and speculation – the enemies of successful change. The rumour mill version of events is almost always worse than reality.... and fear grows. Another, unnecessary, hurdle to success is created: a hurdle that is particularly hard to dismantle.

There is, of course, another way. Recognise up-front that high levels of openness and honesty are the only effective way to keep the rumour mill in check. It is not a sign of weakness to let everyone know at a very early stage that radical change is being considered, but that the full implications are not yet clear. Involve as many key influencers as is practical in all the early deliberations and publicise the main conclusions to-date through them. In recent years we have been astonished by the high levels of morale and loyalty that can be achieved by informing people of possible changes well in advance and requesting their help in the process. This is often true even when the individuals concerned face a significant upheaval in their own personal circumstances through job changes or redundancy.

Once this fundamental philosophy of openness is adopted, the other more detailed design considerations come to the fore. What are the channels of communication between executives and the workforce and vice versa? Which can we control and which are uncontrollable? How do we ensure that the messages we are giving are both consistent and continually reinforce the vision of the business that we wish to create?

In our experience, one of the big surprises you get when you set about identifying channels of communication is the sheer number of them. Once you move beyond the obvious formal channels, such as memos, newsletters, staff presentations and company videos, the range and diversity of communication channels becomes apparent. Consider the following list of less obvious communication channels that often convey the strongest messages to employees:

• The people who have been promoted, in contrast to those that have been passed over, demoted or made redundant.

• The nature of the rewards and remunerations system. Has it been changed to support the proclaimed new objectives, or will the whole idea just blow over? How many compromises have been made to placate the 'old guard'?

• Feedback from ex-employees and friends on the state of the local and national job market. (Rosy visions of people taking responsibility for their own careers, through contract work for example, may need to be seriously qualified if these are not to lose credibility when contrasted with a bleak job market.)

• Performance appraisal feedback. If the work environment is really going to change, how come that my strong interpersonal skills were hardly mentioned and I just got the same increase as Fred, the introvert?

• Why have those people been selected to work on the change design team? And why are we going to be first in attending the change workshops? It all means something.

These, and other informal communication channels, need to be identified and continually cross-checked for consistency and vision implications during a major change implementation.

In parallel, the formal channels must also respond to feedback from non-obvious sources, with messages being adjusted accordingly.

Transitionary channels can also be created to supplement and enhance accurate communications. For example, some leading organisations have used a temporary 'cascade' system of regular meetings at different levels during periods of major change. These meetings are designed to ensure that up-to-date messages and the reactions to these flow both up and down the organisation very rapidly. Opportunities to ask probing questions and receive honest answers are essential if this transient mechanism is not to lose credibility.

There is very little more that needs to be said about channels of communication during periods of change. If you get the philosophy of openness and the channel designs right, you use key influencers, and you are vigilant with message consistency .... it works. But it is a lot more difficult than just writing another pleasantly evasive article for the company newsletter .... and the rumour mill is never totally still.

Forget the fashions, it's 'Total Business Design'

If we are to overcome the piecemeal, often blinkered, approaches inherent in adopting fashionable combinations of business design ideas/tools we need to know what is appropriate to our business and its particular circumstances.

We need some form of simple and effective design tool 'selector': a means of selecting a tool or technique from the many available.

The design tool selector approach that we use has five relatively straightforward steps.

The first step is to identify and prioritise the main business objectives for change. We do this in terms of both competitive advantage and efficiency of operation. In any one year, some companies may choose to concentrate, say, on increasing operational efficiency rather than improving or maintaining competitive advantage, though most try a combination of both.

The second step is to identify which aspects of competitive advantage (innovation, reputation, infrastructure and strategic assets) and efficiency (reduced costs, higher volumes at current costs, fewer faults, faster throughput) are the higher priorities for improvement this year.

The third step is then to match the most appropriate design ideas/ tools against each of the higher priority objectives for the year.

The fourth is to identify specific priority business areas where these design ideas can be effectively implemented.

And the fifth is to spell out the actions needed to progress implementation of the resulting changes in these areas this year.

During this tool selector process, some initial design ideas will be rejected in favour of others that more closely deliver benefits in line with prioritised business objectives.

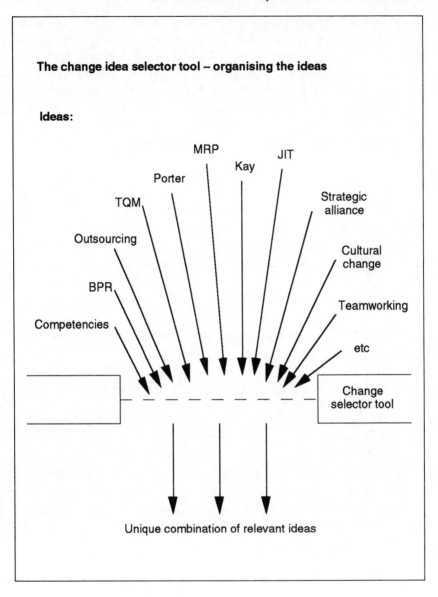

The change idea selector tool – organising the ideas

Ideas:

Unique combination of relevant ideas

Although a fundamental principle of the Total Business Design approach is that senior executives and other key influencers should create and maintain a specific design for each business, we have found that business design educators can be helpful in tuning the design tool selector and in getting the design process started. When a business first starts to use the Total Business Design approach on highly focused, non-standard combinations of design ideas, a business design educator should be used to facilitate a series of workshops where new design initiatives can be created, refined, and selectively put forward for implementation. The educator's knowledge of a wide range of design tools, combined with the participants' knowledge of the business, is a powerful partnership to tackle a seemingly complex, but in reality often quite straightforward, exercise.

The make-up of the workshops is a key determinant of a successful change programme. These workshops all have one thing in common – the creation of a future work environment vision. And workshops with carefully chosen participants and different formats provide unique opportunities to evaluate:

• The likelihood of success in particular change initiatives.

• Potential problem areas, through new work-situation simulation exercises.

• The individuals who are likely to thrive or wilt in proposed new work environments.

In considering this design tool selector approach, it is critical to bear in mind that the selection of much more focused and appropriate design tools does not necessarily guarantee success in business transformation. But it does overcome one significant hurdle. By adopting this approach, new design ideas and tools can readily be incorporated as and when these become available and appropriate. Fashion is thus defeated.

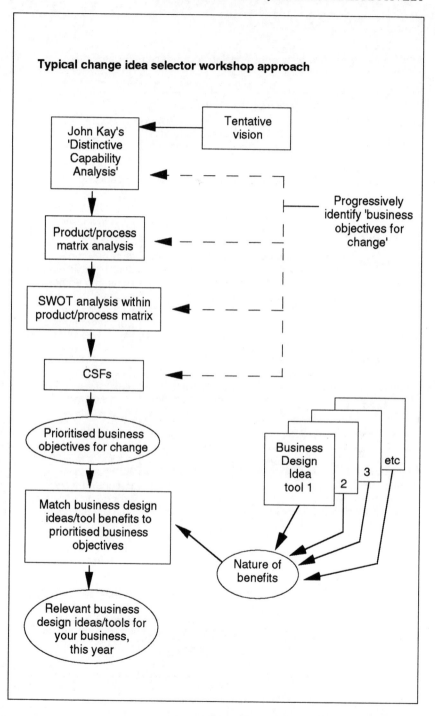

Typical change idea selector workshop approach

Outline examples of business design 'tool selector' (for one year)

Major objectives	Selected, prioritised tools – this year	Revised business design areas (priorities) this year	Actions this year
Competitive advantage Target: To increase overall market share by 5% within 12 months	More innovation	New 'high quality' image product range.	Increased advertising expenditure. New distributor incentive arrange-ments, etc.
	'Strategic asset' consolidation	Expand current brand with high profile, new brand names.	Increased pro-duction facilities. Enter into agree-ments with x and y for exclusive European rights. etc
Efficiency Target: To reduce operational costs by 10% for financial year 1995/96, while maintaining morale levels for core staff	Strategic alliance	For the production of traditional product ranges A and B.	Initiate contacts. Evaluate alternatives. Draft contract options, etc.
	Business process redesign	Accounting/ Finance	Carry out testing through 'simulation workshops'. Complete new integrated work-flow control system, etc.
		Product K cellular manufacturing	Complete final stage of cellular manufacturing for product K.
	Outsourcing	IT data centre and hardware/ network support Personnel recruitment administration	Investigate viability and cost impli-cations, etc.

Change training through practical design simulation

As we mentioned earlier, one of the main 'hurdles' to successful business transformation is the highly variable, and generally poor, quality of relevant training.

Hard training covering traditional skills, such as selling, account management and contract negotiations, is usually tackled reasonably well. And formal training, combined with the use of more innovative approaches (such as coaching and the selective use of mentors) can speed the training of new people in established work environments. However, some of the less routine (and more important) aspects of new unpredictable work environments – such as teamworking and empowerment -- are often major causes of problems. The use of unimaginative, formal training to deal with these soft training needs often generates more heat than light.

At the other end of the spectrum, however, a minority of soft change training is done very well indeed. Imaginative, largely informal training, based on team workshops that simulate different aspects of new work environments, have been used to great effect. We have been particularly pleased with the results of repeated team workshops that take place both before and after a major change, and gradually reduce in frequency as experience of the new work situation builds up. Consequently, we rely heavily on this approach in our change implementation and training designs.

The main mechanics of these innovative workshops are relatively straightforward and can be summarised as follows:

• An introductory session, where the objectives and agenda of the workshop are described to the participants. The objectives are typically to educate those present in the rationale behind the proposed changes, and then to move rapidly on to working out what these mean in terms of real new work situations.

• An issue identification session, where the problems perceived to be the most worrying are identified and put forward for simula-

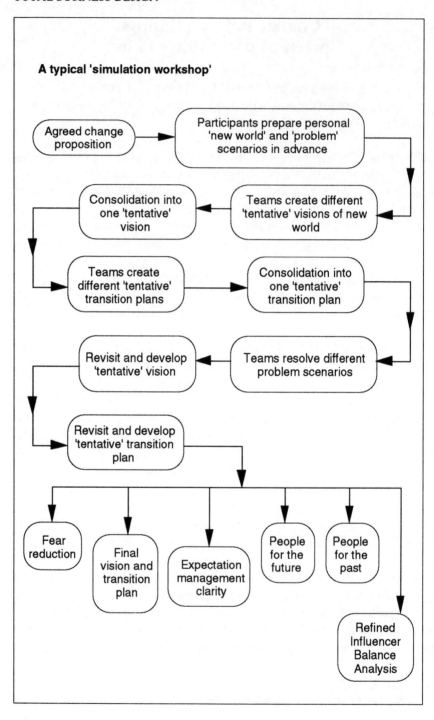

A typical 'simulation workshop'

tion and debate. Generally, the number of issues considered in any one workshop is less than 12, with eight being about the optimum number. The issues are chosen democratically by those present, with the educator ensuring that the mix of issues reflects the interests of all the people attending. The educator also needs to ensure that issues of particular interest to senior executives and other key influencers are included where necessary.

- A series of (often parallel) issue-simulation and debate sessions, where the issues identified can be thought through in the context of the proposed new work environment. The first step in this process is to identify all the relevant aspects of the new environment, such as new working relationships, new computer systems, and new areas of multiskilling/empowerment. The second step is then to test these assumptions (and the specified issues) against a number of potential problems, come to conclusions on possible solutions and wherever possible reach a consensus. Although some of the problems will have been listed in advance by more senior people or by the educator, much of the value of these workshops emerges from considering original problems brought to light by the simulation process itself.

In designing these simulation workshops, educators have a number of variations up their sleeves. For example, a particular issue can be evaluated by different teams working in parallel to cross-check the completeness of the results; or membership of teams can be rotated to spread a common vision amongst participants, irrespective of their particular roles; or particular team combinations can be used throughout the workshop to help build team cohesion; or intractable problems can be revisited by different teams later in the workshop; and so on.

The educator has an important role to play in ensuring that the most appropriate workshop design is used to achieve a particular purpose – at each of the design, implementation planning, and training stages of the change process. The educator also plays a role in introducing problems experienced by other organisations, and by advising when workshops may realistically be reduced in frequency or discontinued as confidence builds.

The principal advantages of the simulation workshop approach (which often includes, but goes well beyond, physical simulation of proposed new processes) can be summarised as follows:

- It extends the theory training into practical realities.

- It identifies solutions to potential problems and highlights gap' in new work design that need further attention.

- It builds a vision of the new environment and how this will function.

- It minimises fear by bringing the new environment to life in the minds of the relevant individuals.

- It builds morale by extensive involvement and by reducing uncertainty.

From a management perspective, the simulation workshop approach also identifies those individuals (at all levels) who will thrive in the new work environment and those who are likely to struggle or resist.

The major drawback of the repeated simulation workshop approach is that it is people intensive and time consuming. However, our experience shows that a few pennies spent on soft training today will save you many pounds in chaos, confusion and failure tomorrow.

Overcoming IT lethargy

Major change has often been delayed or abandoned altogether as a result of problems associated with changing existing computer systems to underpin a new business environment.

Until recently, IT staff have often been torn between doing a 'quick and dirty' job that will require lots of ongoing modifications and expensive support, and spending an unacceptably long time creating large and complex new business application systems.

Fortunately, the IT community is beginning to learn from its mistakes. This gradual enlightenment is being supported by increasing maturity in several of the key enabling technologies and approaches, notably:

- Front-end, client-server technology that can revitalise existing systems. This is achieved by providing a consistent and more friendly user environment through which the old, cumbersome application systems can be activated and controlled. The end result of this pragmatic manoeuvre is to deliver much greater 'horizontal', process-oriented and relevant support to many redesigned business processes.

- Reusable software code that minimises programming effort. Many of the application software packages that have become available in recent years (for applications as varied as production scheduling, financial accounting, personnel records, spreadsheets, process workflow and word processing) are now accessible through a variety of quite sophisticated software tools. These tools can be used to integrate packages into new and different (often horizontal) application systems with minimal programming effort.

- Rapid Application Development (RAD) approaches that speed up the system development process itself. RAD incorporates some quite well-publicised ingredients, such as systems prototyping tools to help the potential users specify their requirements more rapidly and accurately. These RAD approaches, however, also include some powerful project management techniques. 'Timeboxing', for example, has the following characteristics and can be used both for IT projects and (selectively) for other change projects:

- It ensures that each system is specified at the most effective level by close involvement of 'the most senior relevant users'. This builds relationships, clarifies requirements, and minimises 'specification drift' into facilities that would be nice, but are not really urgent or essential.

- It limits the elapsed time for both systems specification and systems development within agreed 'timeboxes' for each project. These timeboxes can vary from a few days to several months in duration. For instance, one very successful formula used in a major insurance company is based on a *maximum* specification period of three elapsed weeks and a *maximum* development period of three elapsed months for delivering a usable system component.

- It uses carefully planned parallel-working schedules, within a self-managed team environment that avoids the need for separate project managers. The approach is significantly enhanced by the availability of multiskilled staff, by a good teamwork culture, and by meaningful incentives for successful quality and timebox completion.

- It optimises the level of system and user documentation by maximising the use of relevant system self-documenting facilities. This avoids both short-term delays and extra costs due to overdocumentation, and future delays/costs due to inadequate documentation.

We cannot stress too strongly that delay is the enemy of effective business transformation. Since IT systems changes are a major source of delay at present, senior executives and other key influencers need to ensure that an effective combination of currently available tools and approaches is used. The objective of this pragmatic exercise should be to get as close as possible to the IT 'holy grail' –

114

rapidly developed, high-quality systems that support transformed businesses.

Some of the best IT people are capable of delivering most, but not all, of this objective today. Many others will just lose their way.

Additional change techniques

Many of the essential change techniques needed for implementing effective business change follow on naturally from our solutions to the four major hurdles (described previously).

However there is a handful of important change techniques that needs further examination. We examine three of these techniques next under the headings of choosing people for the future, getting the motivation balances right and testing viability.

Choosing people for the future

When carrying out a people planning exercise, the first thing we need to do is identify the most likely major business scenarios, say, three to five years ahead; then work out whether these business alternatives will have a significantly different people numbers/ competencies requirement this year. The people requirements picture is then reviewed annually and adjusted as necessary.

The documentation generated by this type of people planning exercise will contain details of people number requirements by competency over time. We have adopted a simple competency categorisation based on:

- *Skills*, primarily technical-type skills.

- *Knowledge*, of particular key aspects of the business or its competitive environment.

- *Behaviours*, such as teamworking characteristics, innovative drives or leadership qualities.

In carrying out people planning, we have found that people numbers and skills are the main outputs. When the resulting actions are initiated, such as redundancies, the recruitment of new people or the transfer of staff to different positions, then knowledge and behaviour characteristics need to be fleshed out.

Evaluating individuals on their knowledge against future requirements is relatively straightforward since most businesses keep records (or relevant personal recollections) of an employee's known knowledge base. Potential employee CVs and the normal interviewing procedures can also extract quite good information on relevant knowledge.

But behaviours are a potential 'can of worms'. While the most obvious high flyers and laggards are easy to identify, the bulk of individuals usually fall into the 'not sure' category. Given a future work environment that no-one knows all the details of, assessing which people will make the grade and which will stumble on the way is far from easy.

Although psychometric tests, teamworking assessments and the like, can give some indication of a person's likely future behaviour, there are severe doubts on the accuracy of these measures during periods of major change.

Research has shown that many individuals faced with high levels of work (and income) uncertainty change their behaviour in line with the new expectations, while being highly stressed and heavily demotivated in the process. This phenomenon is often referred to as the 'survivor syndrome'.

In extreme cases, heavy levels of redundancy can lead to what we call 'survivor trauma'. People suffering from survivor trauma are often incapable of rationally considering further changes for a considerable period of time (sometimes years), even if these changes could improve their own role and economic position.

Within the Total Business Design approach to change management, we have included two techniques that can be used to increase significantly the level of accuracy when predicting which employees will succeed in a new, radically different work environment:

- The first is Influencer Balance Analysis, which combines other influencers' opinions with workshop simulation to provide a quite formal 'new world' assessment of individual executives and other key influencers.

- The second is the assessments of lower-level individuals made informally as a byproduct of the early workshop simulation training exercises. It is much more difficult to hide true behaviours in an intensive two- or three-day workshop than in day-to-day work or formal reviews.

In summary therefore, we recommend that the results of the people planning exercise for the coming year should be implemented by:

- Taking account of relevant individual knowledge levels.

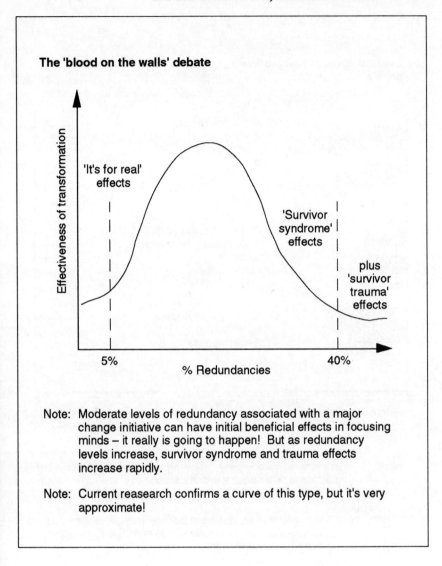

The 'blood on the walls' debate

Effectiveness of transformation (vertical axis)

'It's for real' effects

'Survivor syndrome' effects

plus 'survivor trauma' effects

5%   40%

% Redundancies

Note: Moderate levels of redundancy associated with a major change initiative can have initial beneficial effects in focusing minds – it really is going to happen! But as redundancy levels increase, survivor syndrome and trauma effects increase rapidly.

Note: Current reasearch confirms a curve of this type, but it's very approximate!

- Evaluating senior executives and influencers for the new work environment by using a suitable combination of competency profiles and the Influencer Balance Analysis approach.

- And assessing lower-level people through competency profiles, together with evaluation during simulation workshop training where necessary.

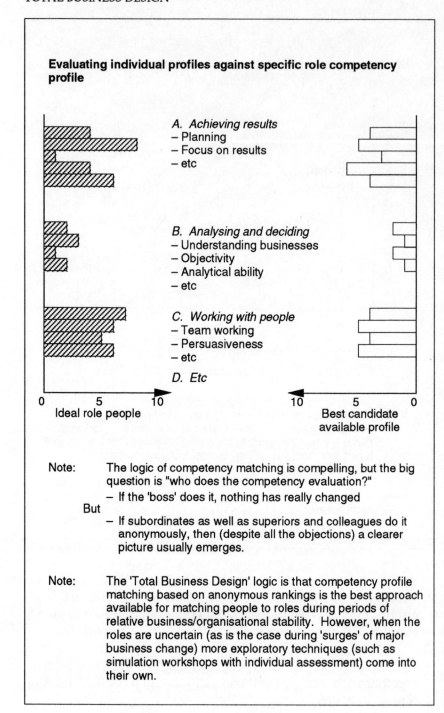

Evaluating individual profiles against specific role competency profile

A. *Achieving results*
– Planning
– Focus on results
– etc

B. *Analysing and deciding*
– Understanding businesses
– Objectivity
– Analytical ability
– etc

C. *Working with people*
– Team working
– Persuasiveness
– etc

D. *Etc*

0   5   10
Ideal role people

10   5   0
Best candidate
available profile

Note: The logic of competency matching is compelling, but the big question is "who does the competency evaluation?"
          – If the 'boss' does it, nothing has really changed
     But
          – If subordinates as well as superiors and colleagues do it anonymously, then (despite all the objections) a clearer picture usually emerges.

Note: The 'Total Business Design' logic is that competency profile matching based on anonymous rankings is the best approach available for matching people to roles during periods of relative business/organisational stability. However, when the roles are uncertain (as is the case during 'surges' of major business change) more exploratory techniques (such as simulation workshops with individual assessment) come into their own.

Experience 10: Six types of competency assessment

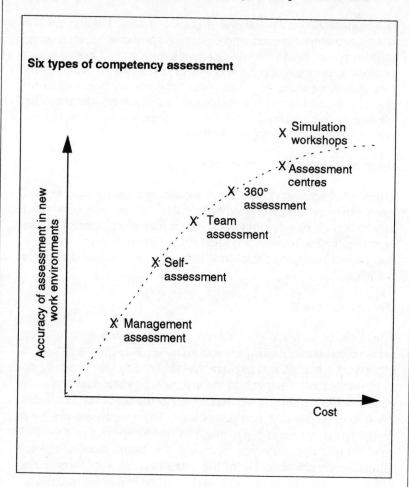

Six types of competency assessment

Management assessment

This is the traditional and most frequently used approach, where an individual's manager carries out the assessment. Although low cost and simple to carry out, this approach is subject to personal bias and has a high error rate in assessing competencies for new, very different work situations.

.../cont'd

Self assessment

This approach uses a variety of questionnaires filled in by the individual being assessed, and is often combined with discussions/agreement on results with the person's manager. One common disadvantage of the approach is that individuals tend to underrate their own competencies. Also, questionnaire wording has to be carefully thought through if reasonably accurate results are to be achieved. The accuracy of predicting competencies for very new work environments is highly variable.

Team assessment

In this approach, individuals are assessed by other members of the team with whom they work. Where necessary, this assessment can extend into other relevant teams where members of those teams work regularly with a particular individual. Once more, however, the accuracy of predicting competencies for key new work assignments is limited.

360° assessment

This type of assessment extends team assessment to include supervisors, senior managers, subordinates and representatives of other work areas, as well as close working colleagues. Typically, up to ten individuals are involved in each selection process, and each assessor fills in a short questionnaire about the individual's performance across relevant competencies. The responses are then analysed to form a composite result and discussed by the individual with the relevant manager. Although this is the most complete, fairest and most accurate of the questionnaire assessment approaches, predictions of future performance in new work environments are still patchy.

Assessment centres

Typically, assessment centres are one-day events designed to identify personal competencies. During these events, individuals carry out various exercises and role plays, together with structured interviews and team exercises. Professional assessors are often

.../cont'd

used. This is more accurate than questionnaire-based approaches, and there is some evidence that it has a reasonable track record in predicting performance in new work environments.

Simulation workshops

These two-day+ workshops are variations on assessment centres that are designed specifically to simulate new work environments. Although in their infancy, simulation workshops are already showing promise as the most accurate predictor of performance in new work situations. In particular, we believe that this approach will become extensively used to select core workers for transformed businesses. Superficially the costs of these simulation workshops look high, but since the results include extensive training and other benefits, as well as individual assessment, the payback per £ spent is often very competitive.

Getting the motivation balances right

If the late quality guru, Dr Deming, was right when he said that only a few per cent of all employees in traditional organisations really enjoy their jobs, then you might legitimately ask the question "does motivation really matter?" After all, businesses of all kinds have continued to function more or less adequately for many decades with largely demotivated people. The pay cheque has always been the one essential motivator. Do you need anything else?

Yet, almost as soon as we ask this question, we instinctively know that traditional levels of motivation – or perhaps, demotivation – are really not good enough. Over the decades, we must have missed huge opportunities to make our businesses more innovative, flexible and responsive to changing customer needs.

We also instinctively know that all motivation is not equally important. Recent research strongly supports this instinct. Also the plain truth is that all employees are not equally important. Our glib phrases about people being our most important asset are long overdue for a bucket of cold water, and a clinical reappraisal.

During periods of major change, we generally witness a wide diversity of both increased and decreased motivation.

At one extreme, those innovative senior executives and other innovative key influencers who initially drive the change are almost universally highly motivated. Often they have been held back by conservative forces over the years and now relish the opportunity to try to change things. Their motivation declines somewhat during setbacks, but while they are 'winning the war' their motivation remains high. However, since only some 5% of business transformation exercises are comprehensively successful, the pattern of motivation for most of these innovators has been highly cyclical in recent years, as they are gradually ground down by less adventurous souls. Interestingly too, the morale of even the most successful innovators has been known to decline once a successful transformation is achieved. Many move on to fresh battles in other businesses, rather than return to the routine business of day-to-day activities, even where these are in very different, reengineered working environments.

At the other extreme, those who are affected by, but not directly involved in, a major change will usually feel apprehensive and motivation levels will be adversely affected. This decline in motivation will, to a greater or lesser degree, depend on the power of the perceived threat to treasured motivational values, such as job security, specialist prestige, or pecking order. Once the surge of business change is introduced (or defeated) the average employee will gradually settle back into a work pattern and the level of anxiety will slowly decline to non-critical levels. This pattern of motivation also applies for those employees who are outsourced or change employer as a result of a change exercise. Once they settle into their new roles, the initial apprehension gradually subsides and motivation rises towards the pre-change (though often abysmal) levels.

Where significant downsizing has taken place, these motivational effects are even more pronounced. Survivor syndrome and survivor trauma effects can seriously damage business effectiveness, while being elusive to identify by traditional management reviews and formal appraisals.

During the recessions of the 1980s/early 1990s, many businesses shed people and were forced to address the impact these changes had on the remaining employees. Outplacement services were extensively used to help those made redundant and the use of these services also had a marginal positive effect on the morale of remaining employees. Those businesses that followed the voluntary redundancy route often found that the most capable people took the money, smiled and ran to another source of gainful employment. The deadwood had to be prised out.

In the midst of all these painful changes, however, the morale of those remaining was primarily determined by the answer to the simple question "what happens next?". New approaches, new challenges and optimism for the future were real tonics to the general levels of morale. In contrast, the sheer grind of taking on ever more work as usual led to predictable, and occasionally severe, morale problems. Sometimes these problems indirectly precipitated the next round of redundancies, as businesses failed in an ever-decreasing vicious spiral of decline, lost business, failure and disillusionment.

Some of the more thoughtful leaders of business change have recently attempted to break through the traditional cycle of low motivation getting lower during periods of uncertainty, and returning to roughly the same low levels as the business situation stabilises. Most of these new approaches to motivation are based on two main principles:

- *Involvement and open communications* to reduce apprehension and treat employees as adults, rather than as children who need to be protected from the harsh realities of working life. In particular, there is a growing trend to make people responsible for their own career development, with the employer collaborating to improve the individual's 'marketability'. In other words, the new employment 'contract' seeks to ensure that the person concerned can rapidly find alternative, suitable employment at any time .... and particularly when, in a changing world, the employer no longer requires his or her services. Traditional job security is replaced by security based on personal 'marketability'.

- *A well understood and fair system for all remuneration*, recognition, promotion and other rewards. For example, one leading management consultancy introduced a remuneration system that balanced the level of individual competency in relevant areas (such as technical skills, interpersonal communications and leadership) with the revenues earned by each consultant during the year. The cumulative 'scores' for competencies and revenues are then plotted on a grid to indicate which remuneration range each individual fell within. Salaries and other benefits are then finalised within the designated range by a conventional appraisal process. We expect this type of system to be adapted and become widely used by innovative businesses. Indeed, some very bold businesses are already using a process where assessment of competencies and performance is carried out by subordinates and peers, as well as by relevant team leaders or managers. This '360 degree' form of assessment is currently the subject of much

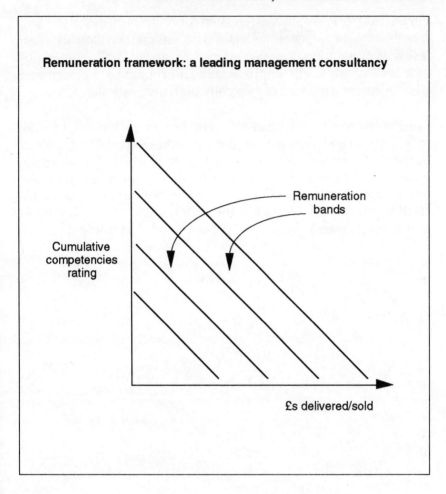

Remuneration framework: a leading management consultancy

Cumulative competencies rating

Remuneration bands

£s delivered/sold

debate. It is also our preferred assessment method for core workers during periods *between* major changes.

Within the Total Business Design approach, we first assess motivation issues by identifying the core employees who are key to the future of the business. For example, in many research and development establishments the employees involved can be categorised into key ideas people, technically skilled scientists and supporting technicians. While the motivation and morale of all employees is important, we weigh the motivation of some as more important than others from a business design perspective.

For the truly core employees, we then concentrate on designing and monitoring the work environment to ensure consistently high levels of motivation, morale and performance. While some individuals will always be unpredictable, it is possible to design and sustain an environment of generally high motivation.

Getting the motivation balances right, however, does not involve following a rigid formula for success. Once again, it's a case of 'horses for courses' and will change over time for all businesses. However, we advocate the principles of treating employees like adults, open communication on all important business issues (including salary levels) and a blatantly fair remuneration, promotion and reward system. Take a deep breath and start doing it.

Testing viability

When you carry out a Total Business Design exercise on your own business, the process will often bear a close resemblance to that well-known video computer game where you drive a car down a racetrack, attempting continually to avoid the obstacles in the way. In our business design game, however, the obstacles include lack of key influencer commitment, 'blood on the walls' constraints, IT systems that are behind the times, the limitations of traditional change training, adopting incidental business fashions, and so on.

Let us assume that you have gone through a Total Business Design exercise along the lines recommended in this book. The vision and designs of your new business world look pretty good, your key influencer balances are now positive in all the important areas, and your change implementation plan has been carefully prepared. It all makes sense but still you have a nagging doubt.... or, at least, you should have one. How do you know you have not missed something? Can you be confident that some change interference effects won't blow the programme off course, or some aspects of one change won't undermine change attempts in other areas. Are we not in danger of just trying to understand too much at once? We need a simple validation technique to check that we have not missed something important.

Fortunately, such a technique does exist. It is quite easy to understand and even easier to use. We call it the 'Business Model Viability Test' and it has two main components.

The first, and higher-level component, examines the business products in the area of proposed change. These 'products' may be real products or services of the business itself, or supporting deliverables produced by different areas of the business, but associated with a final business product. For example, if a proposed change involved buying in and then selling a totally new electronic device, then this would be the final 'product' under consideration. At a lower level, however, we might also examine other deliverables associated with this main product, such as the packaging, the marketing materials, the TV advertising campaign, or the financing options available to customers. At each level we then cross-check for viability against six criteria – business strategy, market intelligence, monitoring, control, coordination and business environment. In effect, we are asking a series of questions aimed at checking the strength of each of these criteria in the proposed new business situation:

- Is the new electronic device consistent with both current and likely future *business strategy*?

- Do we have sufficiently strong market research (*intelligence*) information to be comfortable about the new device's sales prospects during the first crucial year?

- Are the mechanisms that we need to *monitor* the operational performance of the new device ready to be instigated?

- How can we *control* the quality of devices received by our warehouses?

- Are the logistical systems in place to ensure that we can maintain a sound (*coordinated*) balance between variable customer demand in different areas and our related stockholding positions?

- Is the *business environment* likely to change in any significant ways over the next two years? If so, what impact will these have on demand for the new device or its facilities?

The same types of questions may then be asked to cross check viability for, say, the relevant packaging materials or the TV advertising campaign.

This first component, which is based on Professor Stafford Beer's 'Viable Systems Model', is therefore highly focused on the main value-adding processes of the business. By checking all business 'products' involved in change in this way, we can readily identify weaknesses or omissions in the proposed business design against any of the six viability criteria.

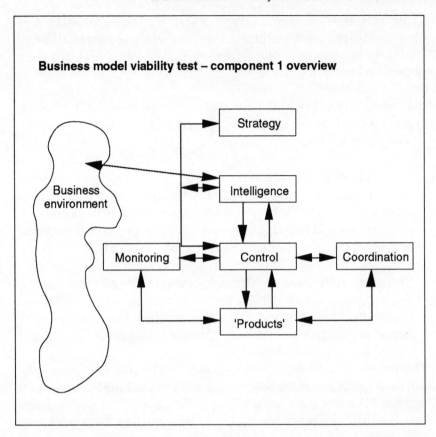

Business model viability test – component 1 overview

The second component of the Business Model Viability Test is much less structured against predetermined viability criteria. Instead, it allows us to check on the cross-impact of any two different aspects of change in a change programme. This is done simply by listing all the different aspects (both design elements and transition actions) of the proposed change in the form of a symmetrical matrix. For any pair of change aspects across the matrix, we then ask the following questions:

- Will either of these changes have an impact (either positive or negative) on the other?

- If so, have we considered the consequences in our designs and implementation plans?

Quite often the results of this type of viability testing produce new insights into the cross-fertilisation or cross-interference of different changes. For example, the following non-obvious findings were obtained during one workshop:

- Proposed changes in the rewards structure to make it "consistently fairer" acted against proposed changes in the focus on 'core' employees.

- Channels of communication during the change process were much more diverse than originally thought. Newly identified channels included interpretations made from promotions, redundancies and role changes; and informal feedback from those employees who were likely to join a local competitor.

- Proposed redundancy patterns (based on innovative/conservative judgements) were likely to cause severe training difficulties in one business process due to a dearth of current customer experience in those remaining after the change.

There is nothing magic or heavily scientific about our viability tests. But then again, few businesses require magic or complex science for success. We use these simply to provide a mechanism for those involved in major business change to check out their own work, and to reduce risks. At the end of the day, the viability tests are just useful frameworks for cross-checking consistency and logic. Business design educators facilitate the process, often by drawing on other Total Business Design ideas to enrich the debate. But the real value is added by staff themselves, who make logical deductions and take different actions as a result of taking part in viability testing.

Business model viability test – component 2 overview

Change issue \ Change issue	No. 1	No. 2	No. 3	No. 4	No. 5	No. 6	No. 7	No. 8
No. 1								
No. 2				cross-check				
No. 3								
No. 4								
No. 5								
No. 6								cross-check
No. 7								
No. 8								
No. 9								
No. 10								
etc								

~ 8 ~
Implementing a practical learning organisation

A 'learning organisation' is potentially the most all-embracing of recent management fashions .... and, perhaps because of its wide scope, it is a source of much debate and abundant confusion.

Most executives have a loose understanding of the underlying logic, along the lines of:

> "Since the business environment is changing faster than ever before, our organisation needs to be constantly learning and adapting. Anything less is a recipe for eventual failure."

But how do we implement a *practical* learning organisation? One that is focused on specific, real business needs; one that can show tangible benefits in the short term, as well as the long; and one that does not cost the earth to install and maintain. Most of the books and conferences on learning organisations have until very recently been less than helpful in answering these simple, very practical questions.

One frustrated chief executive recently said:

> "We have a good training record. We now use a form of competency analysis to identify training needs. What else is there? Will someone please tell me what we do to create a 'learning organisation'? When will we see something significantly different on the bottom line?"

To help all those with a similar (quite reasonable) perspective, we have defined a *practical* learning organisation as one where:

• A cultural environment exists that has a continuing positive balance in favour of beneficial business change. This environment is typified by a constantly evolving, ambitious vision of the business future.

- Mechanisms exist for capturing new change ideas from a variety of relevant sources, both internal and external to the business.

- A form of 'trigger' mechanism exists to channel new change ideas for evaluation, either as continuous improvements or as radical changes.

- Continuous improvement of existing processes and practices is carried out effectively.

- Opportunities for radical change are coherently evaluated and implemented where and when beneficial to the business.

- The possibility of business death and rebirth in different, embryonic forms is an integral part of the overall change culture.

- 'Learning' is selectively designed and focused differently on different people in the organisation.

Let's examine each of these in turn.

A pro-change cultural environment

In any business environment, there will be a natural balance between the level of business ambition and the level of commitment by executives and other key influencers. A learning organisation will strike this ambition/commitment balance at a consistently higher level of change than more conservative businesses.

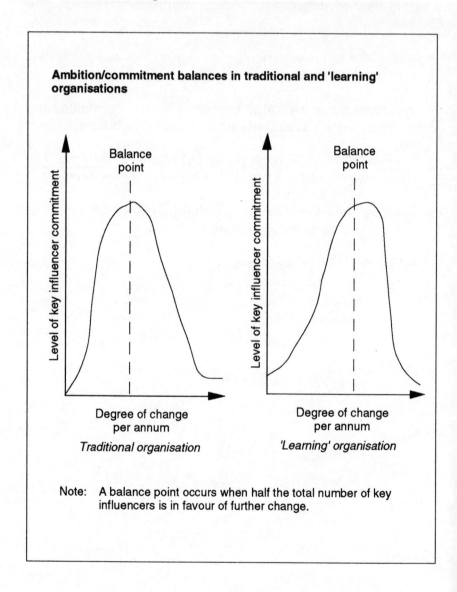

Ambition/commitment balances in traditional and 'learning' organisations

Balance point

Balance point

Level of key influencer commitment

Level of key influencer commitment

Degree of change per annum

Degree of change per annum

Traditional organisation

'Learning' organisation

Note: A balance point occurs when half the total number of key influencers is in favour of further change.

Whether or not the ambition/commitment balance point for any particular organisation turns out to be the most appropriate and beneficial from a business perspective, is, of course, the critical issue. The ultimate judgement will be made with the benefit of hindsight. However, in the short term, a range of obvious measures including market position, profitability, benchmark comparisons with other businesses, and the evaluations made by financial analysts will give some guidance. One of the hallmarks of a successful learning organisation will be that it is capable of adjusting its ambition/commitment balance point to reflect changing business circumstances.

We believe that the Influencer Balance Analysis approach we reviewed earlier and similar approaches will become essential and regularly used within learning organisations. Only be adopting approaches of this type will senior executives be able to assess whether their vision of a business future has the support of a sufficient number of other key influencers.

By definition, commitment (or opposition) to various aspects of business change can only be evaluated where those concerned have a good understanding of the change proposals, the possible side effects, and the likely impact on the overall business and its people. An information culture is therefore a prerequisite for an effective learning organisation. Without openness, learning and subsequent actions will often be misguided, and ultimately futile.

Mechanisms for capturing new change ideas

No learning organisation can thrive without its sources of sustenance – a flow of new change ideas.

While new ideas can be accessed to a limited degree by a process of chance, the really successful learning organisations will have well-thought-out mechanisms for capturing ideas and experiences.

These mechanisms will be tuned to ideas from the broader business world, as well as from the specific marketplace and from within the organisation itself.

Broad business world ideas and experiences can be trawled by, for example, membership of research clubs, by sponsoring academic

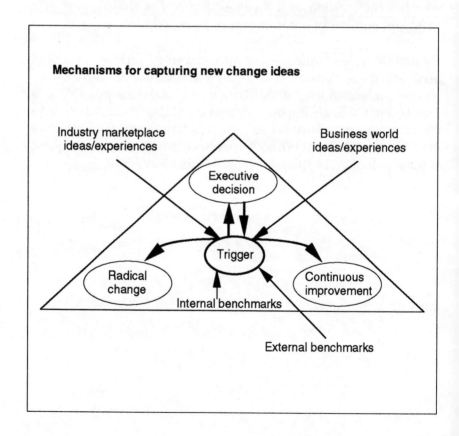

initiates and by maintaining an internal change identification unit. Specific marketplace intelligence on new opportunities and the ways in which suppliers, competitors and customers are improving their businesses can readily be tapped by encouraging and rewarding employees for intelligence gathering. A wide variety of services, including benchmarking services, are also available. Internally, continual improvement programmes and internal benchmarks can be used to identify possible improvements in operations and to act as warning signals on declining standards.

However, effective mechanisms for capturing new change ideas are not, by themselves, enough. These ideas need to fall on fertile ground within the organisation if real change in an acceptable timescale is to result. This fertile ground needs to be prepared in advance, and is characterised by a form of 'trigger' mechanism that sorts ideas into possible and worthwhile improvements and the impossible/worthless/irrelevant.

A 'trigger' mechanism for change

Those would-be learning organisations with an efficient flow of new change ideas and opportunities, from both inside and outside the business, need a trigger mechanism to start the process of evaluation, rejection and selective implementation .

This trigger mechanism is conceptually very simple and usually takes the form of a small (about five-person) task force that is given the job of evaluating all new ideas and opportunities for a period of, say, three or six months. This task force evaluates each idea/ opportunity, rejects those that are either clearly irrelevant or low priority, and passes other ideas into one of three possible change mechanisms – continuous improvement, or radical change to the business machine, or executive-driven radical change – a concept we will explore further.

At the end of the three- or six-month period, new task force members are assigned to the change trigger team. Alternatively, the trigger task force can be changed more gradually to ensure a higher level of continuity. Either way, the aim is to avoid creating a permanent, eventually hidebound, change committee. This can be done by moving individuals into and out of the trigger group at regular intervals. We prefer the gradual rotation approach.

Members of the trigger task force should predominantly be key influencers, or at least individuals with the ability to take a business-wide perspective on change issues. In terms of innovator/ conservative balance, the innovators will usually predominate but always with conservative representation. Both a spread of expertise and suitable teamworking characteristics should be used to select those working on the trigger.

Time spent on the task force will vary but should average at least half a day per week if the exercise is to be taken seriously. The remuneration system will, of course, recognise and reward success-ful participation in the trigger mechanism. Indeed, participation in this mechanism must be seen as a signal of personal recognition and development, and definitely not as a chore.

Mechanisms for continuous improvement

The most effective continuous improvement achievements we have seen have one basic philosophy in common – that the people doing the job are much better placed to see problems and to offer solutions than those in 'management' positions.

Where a self-managed team philosophy exists, those changes can be implemented very rapidly by the instigators once the OK has been given by the trigger task force. In essence, the self-managed team itself has the authority and the budget to make changes in working practices, authorise relevant purchases and change systems. For most continuous improvement suggestions, the trigger task force will only stop or delay a proposed change where there are wider benefits to be gained or where knock-on problems may be caused by the proposed change. The self-management team (and sometimes even an empowered individual) responsible for the process or a process element, decides on all other changes within very broad financial and policy constraints.

Continual improvement works best where it is regarded as a normal day-to-day activity. It fails where a committee culture leads to delays and rejections by those not involved in the specific processes being considered.

While various forms of suggestion scheme and charting of improvement are the trappings of both successful and unsuccessful continual improvement exercises, the number of suggestions, the acceptance rate and the time taken to authorise a suggestion, are all key measures of a continuous improvement environment. A decision-making process that takes more than four weeks is dead on its feet. The best procedures give a yes/no decision within five working days, and have an acceptance rate of more than two-thirds. Management's role in the exercise is to ensure that the mechanism works, to provide encouragement, and to reward successful changes through recognition and tangible reward.

Mechanisms for radical change to the business machine

In the mechanisms for continuous improvement, the trigger task force generally leaves the yes/no decisions to empowered teams or individuals. In stark contrast, however, the decision on whether or not to set up a change team to evaluate and (ultimately) implement a radical change idea rests heavily with the trigger group. A 'yes' decision by this group can speed the uptake of a radical idea. A 'no' decision can kill or seriously delay action.

Once a yes decision to evaluate a radical change idea has been given by the trigger task force, the next step is to establish a change evaluation team. In line with the 'best' implementation mechanism described earlier, this evaluation team should be based on innovative key influencers and will usually consist of about five people with suitable skills/experience/team characteristics working part-time on each change assignment. At any one time, several of these change evaluation teams may be in operation.

Change recommendations are then submitted for senior executive approval. Once the go ahead is given, the techniques of cascading change teams led once again by innovative key influencers is put into operation.

Where the mechanisms of a successful learning organisation are in place, even a radical change idea from a different industry in a far-away country can be captured, evaluated, changed as necessary, and implemented through a highly efficient change management procedure .... in a remarkably short timescale. As a rule of thumb, we believe that businesses following the main approaches recommended in this book should be able to at least halve their major change implementation timescales.

Executive-driven radical change

A range of high-level changes can be carried out by the top executive team without the active commitment or involvement of other key influencers. These changes include downsizing, strategic supplier alliances, business acquisitions and disposals, and new product development.

As a matter of principle, we believe that the top executive team should involve other key influencers in the majority of these decisions, even though these could be implemented in the teeth of fierce opposition by the lower-level key influencers.

Nevertheless, we believe that the trigger mechanism should be designed to give executives the option.

The 'phoenix' option

The possibility of business death and rebirth in different embryonic forms should be an integral part of the change culture in a true learning organisation.

In recent times, we have got used to the reality that businesses change much more rapidly than organisations. A new entrant into a particular market can change a business environment almost overnight through radically different products or distribution channels. But the organisations in that market lag well behind, and are often reluctant to contemplate their own demise. We believe that, in extreme circumstances, even the best organised learning organisations may just not be able to react rapidly or effectively enough to save the business in its current form.

Sometimes these turbulent changes can be anticipated and reasonably orderly transition plans implemented to adjust to a very different business environment. All too often, however, organisations exhibit very human-like qualities and refuse to accept their imminent or lingering demise. Valuable human resources and extensive financial assets can be wasted in vain attempts to regain lost ground, and to reestablish the 'good old days' of only a few years ago.

As always, however, there is another way. A true learning organisation does have one final, radical option as the grim business reaper draws near. We call this 'the phoenix option'. Once the reality of large-scale organisational demise is recognised (or even suspected) senior executives can begin investing much of their remaining business assets in new business opportunities. Sometimes these opportunities will be in the same industry: and sometimes circumstances will dictate that investment in very different types of industry is essential. Businesses as diverse as High Street butchers (being ritually slaughtered by out-of-town superstores) and traditional technical book publishers (seeing a booming new world of computer-based portable multimedia publishing) face the phoenix option today.

It is always worth questioning whether the phoenix option is becoming relevant to your own situation, or whether it may be a useful form of business survival insurance. The phoenix option is often a high-risk strategy – but better than the alternative.

Interestingly, the phoenix option can be deployed by all organisations, not just learning organisations. Change of this kind is in the hands of the senior executive team alone. Other key influencers cannot usually stop, or even seriously delay, the process.

Who will do the learning?

As we prepare for the next millennium, with a variety of different learning organisations in place, considerably fewer people will be directly employed in our enterprises. Several cycles of downsizing, outsourcing, delayering and process redesign will have taken a considerable toll on numbers .... and had a very real impact on efficiency.

But those who remain will be considerably more 'educated'.

The first and most obvious impact of this increased education and training will be that almost everyone will be multiskilled. Multiskilled business process workers will tackle a range of activities and, due to increased empowerment, will directly resolve most of the problems that would traditionally have been passed upwards. These workers will also live in a world where continuous improvements are routine, within the context of very local budget responsibility.

Workers in change/innovation teams will also exhibit multiskilled capabilities at several levels. Those in permanent or semi-permanent teams will be multiskilled in terms of their technical capabilities, such as combinations of scientific skills, IT skills, purchasing skills and marketing/advertising skills. Their general level of training will typically be more specialised and more intensive than that for mainstream business process workers. Nevertheless, much of their work will be process-driven and they too will work in a routine continuous-improvement environment.

Over and above these increased multiskilled levels, there will exist a very different kind of multiskilling. Senior executives, other key influencers, and potential key influencers will constantly be educated in Total Business Design type ideas and techniques. These are the people who will populate the radical change task forces. These are the people who will make the critical judgements on the future of the business. These are the people who will operate in an environment of highly educated 'openness'.

In summary, therefore, if we step back and look at the levels of learning in the new learning organisations, we will see a pattern similar to the following:

- A much higher level of multiskill training and education for all core employees.

- A universal culture of continuous improvement, punctuated by bursts of radical change to both preempt and respond to changing market conditions.

- High levels of education for those 'moving levels' within the organisation – new recruits, process and innovative workers becoming potential key influencers, and key influencers becoming senior executives.

- Very high levels of ongoing Total Business Design type education for all executives and other key influencers.

These are the new cadre of managers who will design learning organisations and who will *use* business design educators, rather than *lean on* traditional management consultants.

Total Business Design, learning organisations and MBAs

At this point in the book, a reader might reasonably ask the question:

"Is Total Business Design really a framework of ideas for a learning organisation?"

The answer is "yes", provided that you also accept that Total Business Design is itself a learning framework. No two businesses will use the framework in exactly the same way .... and the framework itself will be modified, enhanced in scope and improved over time. Each new management idea adds to the Total Business Design framework, from which you and your colleagues can create your own unique and 'tailored' business design.

A few executives, on their first acquaintance with Total Business Design, also ask the question:

"Why can't we simply send our most senior and most influential people on MBA courses prior to creating our own learning organisation?"

Sadly, the answer to this question is "if only". If only the top business schools were able to focus their training to meet your particular business needs .... by using a selector tool of the type we described earlier, for instance. If only they could design their programmes to meet the needs of the different types of core employees – senior executives, other key influencers and continuous improvement, multiskilled workers. If only ......

In reality, however, the trend is in the opposite direction. More and more of the total educational effort is being carried out by businesses themselves, to meet their own specific needs. Those businesses that adopt Total Business Design approaches are likely to reinforce this trend.

~ 9 ~
Using consultants versus DIY

The alternative title of this book "Total Business Design – or how to start taking control of your business's future" pretty well summarises our views on the use of *traditional* management consultants.

This does not mean that successful businesses will never need outside professional help. Indeed, the opposite is the case. True learning organisations are likely to be spending more per head than ever before on research providers, business intelligence, consultant educators and training specialists.

We strongly believe that *traditional* management consultancy has failed Western businesses for two main reasons:

- Reliance on consultants to make their recommendations on business change distracts executives from the real task of doing their own business designs and effectively managing their own change initiatives.

- The quality of management consultants is highly variable. If you find a good one, reliance builds and your emphasis on going-it-yourself is weakened. If you find a bad one, you are no further forward and may well find yourself down some fashionable blind alley.

It is no coincidence that when we examine the relationship between successful economies and declining economies since the Second World War we find the following patterns:

- There is a strong *positive* correlation between expenditure per head on business education/training and business success.

- There is a strong *negative* correlation between expenditure on traditional management consultancy and business success.

Despite the 'cause and effect' arguments that surround findings of this kind, we believe that the lesson is clear. If you are a senior business executive, spend your business's money on consultants who focus on educating your key people. Don't waste it on traditional management consultants who produce worthy reports, but do not gain real commitment.

If you are currently a traditional management consultant, start the metamorphosis into an effective business design educator. Or take up a new hobby. The writing is on the wall.

A major change assignment: Traditional consultancy versus TBD

Traditional consultancy	TBD
Project initiated by executives in response to piecemeal idea or business predicament.	Project initiated as a part of ongoing business change designs based on agreed tool selector results.
Specific design idea dominates the change process (eg BPR, TQM).	Design ideas based on tool selector results of multiple design ideas.
Change teams led by consultants – internal staff used as key workers – influencers involved by chance.	Change teams led by change-educated, innovative key influencers. Consultants educate, guide and facilitate.

.../cont'd

A major change assignment: Traditional consultancy versus TBD (continued)

Traditional consultancy	TBD
Implementation process dominated by logical step-by-step design set up for the purpose.	Implementation process based on balanced view of logical step-by-step design and key influencer balances in particular areas – process is part of well-established change mechanism for both continuous and radical change.
Education on proposed change carried out as part of 'the project' – usually carried out by organisational level at the time and based largely on formal education.	Education on proposed change carried out well in advance for key influencers as part of an 'IBA' exercise. Formal training for others minimised as key influencers + simulation workshops used extensively.
Consultants are well trained in particular design and change management techniques. Good traditional project management skills. They are new to most people working on the project.	Consultants are familiar to all the key influencers in the business in their role of change educators. They are well trained in a range of design and change management techniques, as are the key influencers. The role of the consultant doing specific change exercises is to guide key influencers as *they* put theory into practice.
Changes in business processes, etc lead to changes in people at implementation time.	People changes made once the new business design is agreed – the 'new world' people implement their new environment.

~ 10 ~
Pulling together the
Total Business Design approach

Total Business Design is a flexible, practical framework for a learning organisation. You and your colleagues can accept, reject or modify elements of this framework to create a specific, optimised design for your business. This design will typically include relevant markets, distribution channels and products; organisation and ways of working; people and their motivation; relationships with customers, suppliers and third parties; and the ability of the business to change over time.

The Total Business Design culture is based on lower employee numbers, with much higher levels of multiskilling amongst the remaining core workers. In particular, senior executives and other lower-level key influencers will be educated in the skills and techniques needed to create and implement new designs for their businesses. The quality of the designs, and the ways that these are implemented, will determine to a large degree future business success or failure. The use of traditional management consultants is reduced drastically and the use of business design educators (and other trainers) is heavily increased.

In creating new business designs, senior executives and other key influencers will make use of a design selector tool that will enable them to choose the most appropriate business design techniques for their particular business.

This selector tool addresses the underlying business design techniques, rather than the popular 'fashion' labels, such as Business Process Reengineering or Total Quality Management. New management ideas (and fashions) that emerge over time will also be evaluated using the selector tool. The process gradually becomes second nature. Even the fervent pronouncements of new management gurus are rapidly analysed and put into the context of your own business.

A learning organisation's mechanisms for capturing new ideas are constantly filtering these ideas through a trigger procedure into separate continuous improvement and major change mechanisms.

As businesses move through various cycles of extensive change, punctuated by intervals of relative calm continuous improvement, the Total Business Design approach provides guidance on appropriate actions.

Business design is an ongoing process. The primary role of senior executives is to form judgements on the overall design of the business and to oversee its installation. Other key influencers carry out the more detailed evaluation and implementation work.

Major change occurs as a result of agreed business design changes. Senior executives drive high-level changes, such as big restructuring exercises and business acquisitions. Key influencers at lower levels drive those major change initiatives associated with the business machine itself – once a positive balance of senior executives and other key influencers in favour of each change has been secured.

Continuous improvement decisions are made primarily by those people most closely involved in the business processes being improved. Selected key influencers formed into a constantly rotating trigger task force ensure that the benefits of these improvements are maximised across different work groups, and that any knock-on problems are minimised.

Measurements of key influencer commitment at different levels of business change ambition are monitored and used by senior executives to guide the pace and nature of change through the different change cycles – slow when consolidation is needed, and fast when big opportunities or dangers are sighted. The best executives will be able to tune the change process throughout an organisation, often by close involvement of key influencers at lower levels. All channels of communication, both obvious and non-obvious, are used to facilitate change. And viability tests are carried out regularly to ensure that changes in one area reinforce, rather than interfere with, changes in other business areas.

Change training is used on a 'horses for courses' basis, with a mixture of traditional skills training for hard skills; mixed with simulation workshops for very new work environments; and consolidated by on-the-job training with mentors for new people in established work situations.

The people needed to deal with future business situations are identified and motivated by a combination of:

• Pragmatic strategic planning based on alternative likely business visions that are then used to identify people number and skill requirements – with a strong emphasis on 'what changes will be needed *this year'*.

• Identifying those who also have suitable behavioural attributes – through traditional evaluation combined with simulation workshop assessment.

• Radically new recognition/remuneration structures that go well beyond traditional money-oriented schemes – and concentrate on building individual employability, rather than 'jobs for life'!

The world of Total Business Design in a true learning organisation is a very different world from that in most businesses today. Yet the challenges and benefits of this new world are well within the grasp of most business executives .... providing they have the courage to reject the old ways and to take real responsibility for their own, and their business's, future.

~ 11 ~
TBD: Impact on senior executives

The Total Business Design approach contains both bad and good news for senior executives.

The bad news will confirm what many business leaders already know, or at least suspect. There are some essential aspects of business change that they cannot drive through by themselves – irrespective of how committed, determined and resolute they are.

For some, this realisation comes as a considerable shock. Surely if they are strong enough executives, with drive and plenty of charisma, anything is possible. It seems instinctively right, doesn't it?

Sadly, however, the reality is that the odds against any one executive (or small group of executives) having and being able to use all these characteristics effectively in change situations are overwhelming. Very few of the famous chief executives of our time have achieved success and fame through continually inspiring other key influencers at lower levels in their businesses. It is far easier for a modern executive to learn the rules of the business change game than to acquire large helpings of dynamism and charisma. We believe that learning the rules of Total Business Design is the only effective and practical way forward for a new generation of professional business managers.

The good news behind the Total Business Design message is that, for the first time, executives have a quite simple set of rules that they can use to guide and control all aspects of business change. Dynamism and charisma are still useful attributes, but are not mandatory for a successful outcome. However, resilience and determination, together with knowledge of the rules of the change game, are absolutely essential!

Innovative executives must first accept the latent power of their shadow influencer organisation in driving through or inhibiting change. Next, they must accept objective measures of these shadow influencer balances – remember, an executive's view of key influencers becomes very much less accurate as their day-to-day knowledge of individuals declines. Most executives get the overall list of key influencers about 30% to 40% WRONG. Finally, they must use influencer balance measures to identify viable new change opportunities (brought to light through tool selection and learning organisation mechanisms) and to selectively implement relevant changes using key-influencer-driven change procedures.

Once professional executives have accepted the constraints and opportunities presented by Total Business Design, a whole new insight emerges. For the first time, they can pull the strings of the shadow change mechanisms. Rather like a skilled puppet master, they are really in control. They can establish suitable processes for different types of change and fine tune the mechanisms for radical, moderate or nil change in any part of the business at any point in time.

Where radical change is needed, innovative influencers are introduced and blockers removed, leading to a strongly positive balance in favour of change. Where more modest change is needed, a more even balance between innovative and conservative influencers will deliver the desired result. And where a steady hand is needed to maintain the status quo, or to consolidate after a major change, it is the turn of the innovative influencers to be moved to other positions. While any process of change will have its casualties, this professional horses for courses approach to change management will typically result in much less personal grief than the more traditional (80%+ failure) methods. The principle used throughout this new change management process is to adjust the influencer balances *before* the change, or consolidation, starts. The right type of influencers will then drive the necessary process and system changes with a minimum of political infighting.

Regular Influencer Balance Analysis becomes the crucial measure of all the things you really need to know:

• What is possible, and not possible, with existing influencers?

- Which influencers do you need to convert or remove before you can achieve the objectives?

- How are you doing at any point in any change initiative?

Luck is minimised, but courage is needed. Insecure executives will avoid the real issues. Fear that others may rate them poorly in terms of influence or innovation are very real. Initially, only the most courageous dare to measure their shadow organisation .... and thereby selectively drive effective, major change. However, we believe that the success that results will create an unstoppable momentum. Business executives will be in charge in a way that their autocratic predecessors never were – despite the bluster. The age of the truly professional business executive will have arrived .... driven by a business design that is total, yet able to identify and absorb relevant new ideas in future.

Influencer design overview

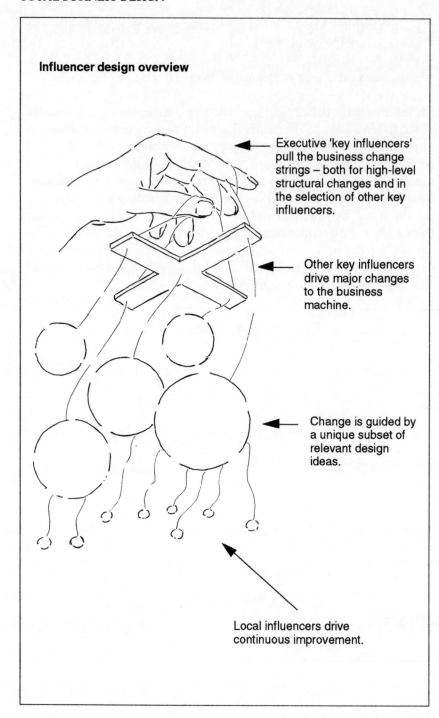

Executive 'key influencers' pull the business change strings – both for high-level structural changes and in the selection of other key influencers.

Other key influencers drive major changes to the business machine.

Change is guided by a unique subset of relevant design ideas.

Local influencers drive continuous improvement.

~ 12 ~
TBD: The three convergences

In this book we have explored the underlying reasons for the very poor results of most business transformation attempts. In stark contrast to almost all management gurus, who have focused on apparent successes, we have primarily analysed failure – and have used the lessons learnt from these failures to put the rare successes into a very different context.

The result, we believe, is to add an extra dimension to the often fashion-driven business approaches in general use today. No current or future business design or change management idea is beyond the scope of Total Business Design. The TBD model is very powerful and represents a major step forward in the maturity of management thinking and business practice.

The prime objective of the TBD approach is very simply to minimise the risk of failure in business transformation of all types .... to change the 80%+ failure rule into the 80%+ success rule!

As the book has evolved we have become more and more prescriptive, while avoiding the pitfalls of developing a fixed and rigid methodology. Indeed, the greatest danger of the Total Business Design approach is not that it is too narrow or too inflexible. The danger lies at the opposite extreme – for some, there are just too many concepts and insights to be absorbed and applied in real business situations .... at least without some rules of thumb to guide them on the way.

Human beings like to use rules of thumb to cut across complexity, without losing any of the essential elements of new approaches. We have therefore summarised the essence of the TBD approach in three rules of thumb that we call the *three convergences*.

The first TBD convergence is the convergence of all business design ideas through a matching process to meet the needs of your specific business this year. A subset of all possible design ideas is chosen by matching the objectives of these ideas to the specific current objectives of the business. To help create a mental image of this process, we have used a picture of a sieve to illustrate the reduction of possible business design ideas into the chosen (and relevant) few.

The second TBD convergence is that between business change management processes of all types, ranging from ongoing continuous change through to radical change – and including the mechanisms necessary for identifying and implementing business change in future (often called learning organisation mechanisms). The essential ingredient necessary to make this convergence work in a rational and practical way is the use of key influencers as the driving force behind all change initiatives within the business. Because key influencers are typically scattered throughout the organisation with higher densities in more senior positions, we have used an illustration of this type. Since there is often a significant mismatch between business organisation charts and key influencer charts, TBD change management is very different from almost all traditional business transformation initiatives.

The third TBD convergence is the convergence, or merger, of management education with management consultancy. Because key influencers (and not organisation chart 'executives' and 'managers') are the prime mechanism for successful change in a business, the most effective change education is that which is clearly focused on these influential people. (Since a typical strategic business unit will have a maximum of 30 to 40 key influencers, this approach can be highly economic as well as very effective.) High-quality, up-to-date and innovative influencer education – covering relevant aspects of business design and change management as identified by the matching process described above – can create very fertile ground for all business change. However, this fertile change environment is necessary, but not sufficient, for achieving a very successful change record over time. The most successful businesses at the end of the millennium will be those that coordinate their key influencer education with consulting services that provide top-quality guidance and help key influencers during change processes. A new breed of consultant/educator supplier will gradually emerge to meet this hybrid need, and we will witness the decline of both

TBD: The three convergences

Convergence 1

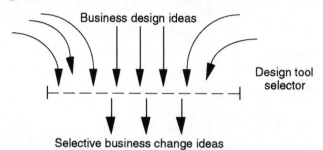

Business design ideas

Design tool selector

Selective business change ideas

Convergence 2

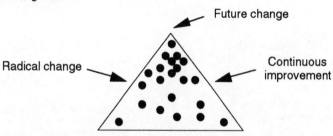

Future change

Radical change

Continuous improvement

Different types of Key Influencer drive different types of business change under a single integrated design

Convergence 3

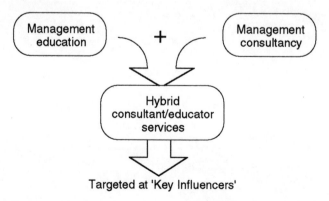

Management education

\+

Management consultancy

Hybrid consultant/educator services

Targeted at 'Key Influencers'

traditional piecemeal management education and management consultants who 'recommend' change, rather than help the key influencers to get the job done.

We believe that these three TBD convergences provide an essential rule-of-thumb set for all ambitious business influencers in the late 1990s.

Good luck!

~ 13 ~
Twenty questions and answers about Total Business Design

We have compressed a lot of insights, information and opinion into this Total Business Design book. Needless to say, we made extensive use of the simulation workshop approach in our attempts to be both comprehensive and brief. Despite this, we knew that many questions would remain outstanding.

As we neared completion of the book, we therefore circulated a draft to a cross-section of 500 senior executives for comment. Of the 42 individuals who responded, some agreed to go 'on the record' – their comments are given in Appendix C. Others, however, made comments and raised a series of questions 'off the record'. We have consolidated these questions, with our answers, in this section. With a few exceptions, the response to the book and the tone of the questions asked were extremely positive.

Question 1:
" In browsing the book, I note that you have covered a lot of familiar techniques. What is really new?"

We set out to explain why so many well-intentioned business transformation initiatives fail to achieve initial, often radical, objectives. In doing this, we described the scope and limitations of many of the business design techniques that are in the public domain (and familiar to some readers). Quite often, however, our views are at odds with most current opinion.

We believe that many aspects of our proposed solution to major change problems are original and represent real steps forward from current practice. For example, the Influencer Balance Analysis approach enables even non-charismatic business leaders to gain control of major change initiatives; and our approaches to change tool selection, implementation management, viability testing, and simulation of new work environments goes well beyond almost all other existing techniques.

Question 2:
"Does the high failure rate for transformation of the business 'machine' also apply to large IT projects?"

The answer is almost certainly 'yes', although our research on this issue is not yet far enough advanced for us to give a definite answer. At present, our best judgement is that large IT projects have a poor track record (but not as bad as the disastrous history of business transformation) and that people factors very similar to those discussed in this book have the single biggest influence on success or failure. We believe that the use of Influencer Balance Analysis techniques will notably enhance the effective project management of large IT projects.

Question 3:
"What is the lowest number of key influencers for which you would recommend use of the Influencer Balance Analysis technique?"

In practice, formal IBA exercises are likely to be an overkill where there are fewer than (say) eight key influencers. In relatively small areas of change, it is much more likely that the main change agent(s) are familiar enough with the individuals concerned to be able to carry out influencer balance calculations without a formal exercise.

Indeed, even in large change exercises it is possible to assess influencer balances informally. At one of our clients, for example, the main change team carried out an informal commitment evaluation by polling only the views of identified change agents at all levels until a reasonably consistent picture of the likely 'blockers' emerged. The main change team then carried out a rough influencer balance exercise based on their opinion of the relevant weightings and focused their attention most onto potential problem areas.

Question 4:
"Have you not been too hard in your assessment of business transformation failures? What criteria do you use for real success?"

Undoubtedly, our criteria for success were very tough. In essence, for commercial organisations, we classified a major success as one that would be visible to shareholders in the short or medium term and would have a significant impact on the chief executive's reputation (both within and outside the business). Similar criteria were applied to government bodies. We really felt the need to act as an antidote to much of the 'rose-tinted spectacle' analysis that abounds in the business transformation area.

Question 5:
"How would you recommend that an average business should start on the road to Total Business Design?"

Identify the key influencers in your current business environment. (Typically, there will be about 30 people in total for each significant strategic business unit.) Then arrange for them to be educated in business design and change management techniques, without any formal preconceptions as to how these techniques might be applied in your business.

Only at this point are you in a position to start creating new business designs, evaluating influencer balances, and planning your changes along the lines described in this book. Use consultant 'educators' to help you in this process .... and remember that they can help, but they can't do it for you.

Question 6:
"Why have you omitted discussion of an integrated marketing/ operations strategy to create and then respond rapidly to customer needs?"

In some businesses, working for example in fashion-led markets, this type of dynamic relationship between marketing and operations is critical to success. However, we were determined to write a short book that would be used by senior executives in all businesses, and we had to leave some interesting issues out.

Question 7:
"You are very harsh on traditional management consultants. Is this just a popular form of 'kick the cat'?"

OK, management consultants have had a bad press and are, to some extent, an easy target. In criticising the way that most management consultants have operated up to now, our main objective is to stress that senior executives and other key influencers must own, live, eat and breathe their business changes. A heavy reliance on management consultants who recommend specific changes usually operates in direct opposition to this key prerequisite for success in business transformation.

Educated key influencers are in the best position to design and implement successful business change. The role of the consultants is to provide the education, not the recommendations!

Question 8:
"We have recently implemented a number of major changes to our business operations. To a considerable extent, many of the initial bottom line benefits have been achieved. Yet morale across the business seems to be pretty low. What should we do?"

This is a very common scenario and one where it is all too easy to make the wrong diagnosis. The most optimistic prognosis is that all is well with your change programme and you are simply experiencing the (almost) inevitable short-term dip in morale that is a reflection of quite natural concern about even the best designed and managed change exercise. Things will settle down in weeks rather than months and a communal glow of satisfaction will steadily emerge as fear disappears.

The worst prognosis is that almost everything is wrong with your change initiative. Limited early optimism in the workforce has turned to widespread cynicism and outright despair in some areas.

Major elements of the new designs are clearly wrong for your business, the new IT systems just don't work, the people factors have been badly mishandled and the new business vision is viewed as a joke. Good people are scanning the recruitment columns and someone has even opened a book and is laying odds on how long the chief executive will hang on to his current job.

The truth is almost always somewhere in the middle of these two extremes. Your curate's egg of a change process can probably be refreshed without too much pain or additional cost. But don't leave it too late. Your instincts on the state of affairs are probably reasonably accurate, but if the symptoms persist for more than four to six months call in a new doctor for a second opinion.

Question 9:
"You recommend a number of specific approaches in the book. Are you falling into the trap of being too prescriptive?"

We sincerely hope not. Any and all of the specific techniques we advocate in the book (such as the Kay model, role/competency profiles, remuneration frameworks, viability testing and the Hersey/Blanchard framework) are dispensable. Indeed, we would be extremely surprised and disappointed if significant improvements in these techniques were not forthcoming over the next few years. Just use the techniques we advocate as benchmarks as you work on your own alternative business designs. The one approach that we expect to remain reasonably consistent over time is the essential TBD model .... based on the essential learning organisation ingredients of design tool selection and effective, key-influencer-led, change implementation.

Question 10:
"Do you use Influencer Balance Analysis for just the overall (and individual) key influencer ratios, or can you extract more detailed information from the process?"

We do extract quite a lot more from the results of a typical Influencer Balance Analysis exercise. For instance, we can carry out a sensitivity analysis for both positive and negative ratios to determine how resistant these ratios are to marginal changes in support/opposition to specific changes. We can also identify those individuals who are most in need of further education/motivation, even where the overall balances are strongly positive.

Question 11:
"In the book, you have suggested a pretty universal approach based on standard wisdom modified by business-specific focusing. Is this so, and do you believe that there are any big areas of standard business wisdom that have yet to be uncovered?"

We believe that the learning organisation concept of gaining publicly available wisdom and modifying this for individual businesses is very powerful.

New areas of business wisdom will definitely continue to be created. The whole area of centralisation/decentralisation, for example, has proved remarkably resilient to definitive analysis over the years. At the moment, we are very interested in examining the most 'natural' organisational arrangements for delivering effective and efficient customer service in a variety of different situations, ranging from banking and insurance services through maintenance services for utilities to the emergency services. Technological change and changes in the different market environments are raising fundamental questions on the 'best' organisational arrangements.

Question 12:
"How does the Total Business Design approach explain the ability of, for example, Microsoft to overtake IBM as the dominant force in the IT market?"

Superficially, quite simply. In retrospect, IBM seems to have presented Microsoft with one of John Kay's strategic assets (the de facto operating system standard for personal computers) on a plate. We bet it didn't seem that way at the time though!

Question 13:
"You have skipped over the quality movement very rapidly. Is this really logical, and have you missed some important elements of best business practice?"

We were determined to make the point that the quality movement needs to be viewed in the context of both continuous improvement and radical business change. In doing this we doubtless skipped lightly over a wide range of best practice approaches. Our apologies go to all those who are gaining real business benefits from the work of Deming, Juran, Crosby, Feigenbaum, Ishikawa, Garvin, Shingo, Taguchi, etc.

Question 14:
"Can businesses really foresee the future? In my experience most of the really big changes in business markets happen too quickly to be planned for in 'learning organisations'."

Although 20:20 vision of the future is certainly extremely rare and probably non-existent, we know of numerous businesses that are succeeding in the 1990s by adopting a realistic, not idealistic, view of their future business world. (We also know of almost as many business people who have looked at the future through rose-tinted spectacles and are now very cynical indeed.)

Question 15:
"Can 'networked' organisations where most of the real value-added comes from subcontractors of one sort or another survive in the medium and long term?"

You have identified the critical issue. Where a networked organisation provides real value added over a period of time, it has the essential prerequisite for survival. However, where market situations change and little value is added as a result, associates or competitors are highly likely to change the business rules with terminal effect.

169

Question 16:
"In viability testing, you stress the importance of possible negative impacts between one change and another. Is this likely to be a major problem in most cases?"

Interference between one change and another becomes more likely as the number of changes attempted at any one time increases. This type of interference is therefore quite common in large change exercises and relatively rare in smaller ones. Watch out for different types of interference effect .... from the obvious situations where inappropriate or delayed new IT systems can have profoundly negative effects on new organisational arrangements, to more subtle problems created by sending conflicting messages to employees as a byproduct of separate change activities.

Question 17:
"Can the motivation of professional workers ever really survive the downgrading of their professional career paths?"

There are many examples where motivation increases substantially as new challenges are accepted. We speak from personal knowledge as two individuals who left thriving traditional 'careers' to set up new businesses. We also believe that this fundamental change is an essential part of being a 'professional' as we near the end of the millennium. However, as a general conclusion, the jury is still out.

Question 18:
"What will the impact of 'effective' business transformation be on unemployment levels?"

We predict that the advanced change management techniques now available will have a considerable impact on employment levels in large businesses, perhaps leading to an eventual decline in employee numbers of some 20% to 30% of current (post-downsizing) levels. However, since most people in Western economies work for smaller businesses, the impact on general unemployment levels will be significantly diluted. The most significant trend, however, is for increased demand for skilled and multi-skilled workers at the expense of the unskilled. The unemployed and under-employed residue of the workforce in Western economies will increasingly be characterised by the unskilled and the 'narrow skilled', made redundant from traditional functional jobs.

Question 19:
"Will people effectively take control of their own 'employability', or is this just an excuse used by employers avoiding their historic responsibilities?"

We expect this transition to be a difficult one. Certainly, most employers will need to be considerably more imaginative than they have been up to now if 'employability' is to become the basis for successful work relationships.

Question 20:
"What do you think of Tom Peters' ideas of businesses following a policy of 'continuous revolution'?"

We regard the Peters' approach as very much a simplistic two-dimensional solution to a three-dimensional problem. All businesses need to continuously improve. All businesses need to make radical changes from time to time. Very few businesses indeed need to implement 'continuous revolution'! The overheads are just too great .... and few can dodge the law of diminishing returns.

~ 14 ~
Postscript

Almost all of the transformation and change management ideas described in this book have been used in real businesses. However, to the best of our knowledge, no one business has yet implemented all the elements of Total Business Design.

If you are interested in moving in this direction, the authors of this book (Neil Farmer and Bob Lankester) would like to talk to you.

UK Telephone: 0171 831 5262

UK Fax: 0171 242 0011

~ Appendix A ~
Influencer Balance Analysis
–Educators guide

(This is an edited extract from our business design
educator's handbook. The handbook has been
refined from practical experience.)

Introduction

Before carrying out an Influencer Balance Analysis (IBA) exercise,
we must have a change (or 'no-change') proposition, together with
objectives and rough details of the implications. We also must have
senior level support for the IBA project.

Stage 1 : Initial interviews

1. Select starting point(s) of key executives / influencers – start
   with obvious relevant influencers.

2. Carry out face-to-face interviews starting with the most senior
   individual, to determine :

   – The key influencers in the area of proposed change (this is an
     upwards, sideways and downwards review).

   – The relative 'weighting' of these influencers *in terms of influ-
     ence in achieving/blocking change.*

   – The positional 'balance' of these individuals on a generic
     innovator/conservative 10-point scale.

3. Repeat this exercise until a reasonably consistent picture of key
   influencers, their areas of influence and their positional balances
   emerges. (Note: It may not be necessary to interview all the
   influencers at this stage – we can stop once a consistent picture
   is established. As a rough guide, if 30 executives/influencers are
   identified, we may need only 10–15 interviews before a high

level of confidence is established in the result, due to a consistent picture emerging from diverse sources.)

4. Use this interviewing process to gather additional relevant information on the business activities/processes, etc, associated with, or influenced by, the proposed changes.

Stage 2 : Workshop group selection

During this brief second stage, we identify the most logical and practical division of individuals into workshop groups. Further 'rules of thumb' for this exercise include :

– Do not mix 'executives' with 'influencers' in any workshops.

– Split the executives into at least two workshop groups to reduce any individual dominance effects.

– Similarly, mix influencers of similar 'power' wherever possible.

– The optimum workshop number is eight participants; small enough for group discussions, yet with the capability of creating two teams of 4 people for specific exercises during the workshop.

– Allocate a different educator to each workshop (as far as possible) to minimise overall educator bias.

– Mix innovators with conservatives, wherever possible building in an positive innovative balance. The objective here is to ensure that most workshops have a positive balances, even if this means that one workshop is heavily negative.

Stage 3 : The initial workshops

Ideally, each workshop lasts for 4 days in a pleasant off-site venue. Administrative support is provided to ensure rapid creation of typed material and to ensure venue efficiency in support services.

The first day is typically devoted to participant induction and education. The initial induction session clarifies the objectives for the proposed change and the deliverables from the workshop exercises and other aspects of Total Business Design implementation. The education session brings participants up to speed with the business design tools that are considered particularly relevant to their specific business and areas of proposed change. Make sure you clarify the thinking behind the 'design tool selector' approach.

The next two days of the workshop are spent 'designing the new world' in more detail using the selected tools. During these exercises, we make extensive use of situation simulation to test new ideas against realistic work structures.

The objective of these two days is to build up some of the key details of the relevant business environment after the proposed changes are implemented.

The final day of the initial workshop is focused on the actions that need to take place to implement the proposed changes, together with appropriate timescales.

During the final 30 minutes of each workshop, participants fill in an influencer balance questionnaire, expressing their opinions on the levels of individual support for each significant aspect of the proposed change. (In other words, this builds on the 'positional balance' information gathered during the initial interviews, but provides insights into personal commitment at a more detailed level.)

The end products from the initial workshops are therefore a series of medium-level visions of the new business environment, together with a variety of proposed actions plus timescales; and the all-important influencer balance analysis for each significant aspect of the proposed change.

Stage 4: The reconciliation/gap analysis workshop

Ideally, this workshop lasts for 2 days. The inputs are the various visions and actions generated by the initial workshops. The objective of this stage 4 workshop is to reconcile, as far as possible, the different visions/actions into a coherent agreed plan of action – for positive balance changes.

During this workshop, all initial workshops participants (or at least a representatively large sample) will take part. The first part of the workshop (1/2 day) will be used to explain all the suggested visions/actions to participants. Approximately 1 day will be used to discuss the propositions using smaller group iterations, supported by our administrative people. The final 1/2 day will be used to create the agreed plan of action, positive and negative balances etc. Remember that negative balance proposals are also an important deliverable from this reconciliation exercise – these gaps in opinion will need to be overcome before progress on negative balance visions/actions can be made. Avoid glossing over the differences in the heat of the moment.

Getting the influencer balances right

In evaluating the influencer balances obtained from the interview and workshop processes, our objectives are as follows:

- To identify those areas of change where there is a sufficient positive balance of innovators to give a high probability of successful implementation. (A weighted positive balance of greater than 2:1 is comfortable; at 1.5:1 or worse, something needs to change.)

- To identify those areas of change where there is not a sufficient positive balance of innovators to indicate successful implementation. In these cases, we evaluate how important each area of change is to the overall change programme and its objectives. If the area of change is not very important, consider dropping it from the change programme (at least in the short term). If the area of change is important in the context of the overall change programme, then examine the options for adding new 'innovators' into relevant influential positions, or moving out some of the 'conservatives' currently in influential positions.

These changes should be made before the relevant changes are attempted. Also, watch out for overall 'blood on the walls' balances to avoid survivor syndrome and survivor trauma. Leave a minority of sceptical influencers in place to temper the more unrealistic, zealous advocates of change.

- To identify and agree on the logical change implementation plan in the light of the influencer balances achieved.

~ Appendix B ~
Businesses we researched

Name	*Area of interest*
Aer Lingus	Strategic alliances
Aetna Life & Casualty	IT BPR
Aid Associations for Lutherans	Teamworking/reward schemes
Air France	Core business concepts
Alamo Car Rentals	BPR
Alcoa Manufacturing	Radical step change
Allied Dunbar	BPR
American Airlines	BPR
American Express	Credit authorisation PR/ empowerment
Analog Devices	Learning organisation
Anglian Water	Restructuring/BPR
Asea Brown Boveria	Change initiative
AT&T	Reorganisation into smaller network of organisations
Automobile Association	Customer focus
Avery International	Innovative marketing/ strategies
Avis	IT-led BPR
Avon	Global markets
Banca d'America e d'Italia	IT-led BPR
Banca Popolare	IT process redesign
Bank of Scotland	BPR
Barclays Bank	BPR
Barr & Stroud	BPR
BASF	BPR
Bass	Core business concepts
BAT Industries	Strategic alliances
Baxi Partnership	BPR
Baxter Healthcare	Process redesign
Benetton	BPR/IT client server

Name	Area of interest
Birmingham Midshires	BPR Building Society
Black & Decker	Global strategy
BMW	Learning organisation
Boeing	Core business concepts
Bosch	Widespread teamworking
BP Oil Australia & NZ	BPR and BP simplification
Brandywine Corporation	Teamworking
Brent Council	Customer focus
British Airways	Change initiative
British Alcan Aluminium	'Patchwork' BPR
British Broadcasting Corporation	BPR
British Gas	BPR
British Nuclear Fuels	TQM and 'process involvement teams'
British Rail	Customer-focused process redesign/BPR
BT	BPR
Cable and Wireless	Strategic alliances
Cadbury Schweppes	BPR
California State Automobile Association	BPR
Cambridgeshire County Council	Outsourcing
Campbell Soup	BPR
Canon	Multiskilling
CBS/Fox	BPR
Chaparral Steel	Learning organisation
Chemical Bank	BPR
Chevron	Human resource strategies
Chrysler	BPR
Chubb & Son	BPR 'Change at Chubb' programme
Churchill Potterny	Process redesign
Ciba UK	Empowerment measurement
Cigna International UK	BPR
Cin-Made Corporation	Empowerment/profit-sharing scheme

Name	Area of interest
Citibank	BPR
Coca Cola	Continual improvement programme
Colgate-Parmolive	BPR
Compaq	BPR
Cosalt Holiday Homes	TQM
Department of Trade& Industry	'Best practice' in small and medium sized organisations
Deutsche Telecom	Strategic alliances
Digital Equipment Corporation	Supply chain, IT-led BPR
Digital South Pacific	BPR
Direct Line	BPR initiative underpinned with MIS redevelopment
Dominion Insurance	IT-led BPR
Dow Chemical	Regional strategies
Du Pont	IT-led BPR
Duracell	BPR
Eagle Star Insurance	Process redesign
Elf Atochem	BPR
Elida Gibbs	Process orientation
Enron	Client server/process redesign
Equity & Law	Outsourcing
Exxon Chemicals	Process orientation
F International	Employee ownership; shamrock organisation
Federal Express	Empowerment
Fiat	Strategic alliances
Foodmaker	Outsourcing/core employee concepts
Ford Motors	BPR
Frizzell Financial Services	Empowerment
Galileo International	Strategic alliances/ advanced IT strategy
Gateway Foodmarkets	Process orientation
General Electric Comany	Boundaryless company

180

Name	Area of interest
General Motors	Strategic alliances/BPR
Glaxochem	Customer-supplier initiatives
Golden Wonder	BPR
Grand Metropolitan	Decentralisation into smaller SBUs
GTE	BPR
Guinness	Process redesign
Halifax Building Society	Innovation
Hallmark Cards	BPR
Hazleton Washington	BPR
Heineken	Pacific-rim strategy
Heinz Company	"Customer's customer" view
Hewlett-Packard	BPR
Hitachi	Reorganisation
Honda	Strategic alliances
Horion Travel	Process redesign
Hyundai	Strategic alliances
IBM Credit	BPR
IBM UK	Reduction of functional layers
ICI	Mergers
ICL	Supplier evaluation
Ikea Furniture	Supplier strategies
Industrial Bank of Japan	Team building
ITT	Strategy
J P Morgan	BPR
Johnson & Johnson	Scaled-down operations
JVC	Pacific-rim strategy
Kelloggs	Reputation/brand strategy
Kingston Hospital NHS Trust	'Investment-in-change' programme – BPR
KLM Royal Dutch Airlines	Strategic alliances
Kodak	Radical restructuring
Kraft General Foods	Cultural change
Legal & General	'Projects for improvement'/ teams

Name	*Area of interest*
Leicester Royal Infirmary	BPR
Lever Brothers	Empowerment
Libby Associates	Manufacturing BPR
Liquid Carbonic Industries	BPR
Lloyds Bank	BPR
London Rubber Company	Client server/BPR
Lowenbrau	Core business concepts
Lucas Industries	Benchmarking
LVMH	Reputation/brands
Marks & Spencer	Business review of information process redesign
Marlow Industries	TQM Council
Mars	Brands
Mazda	BPR
McDonalds	Franchise strategy
Mercedes Benz	BPR
Mercury Communications	BPR
Microsoft	Strategic alliances
Midland Bank	Strategy
Milk Marketing Board	BPR
Milliken	TQM (European Quality Award 1993)
Motorola	Reward systems/BPR
Mutual Benefit Life Insurance	BPR
National & Provincial Building Society	BPR push, concentrating on non-IT change
National Express Coaches	Core business concepts
National Freight	Employee participation
National Vulcan	Major IT-led BPR programme
National Westminster Bank	BPR
Nationwide Building Society	BPR
Navistar International	Competitive change programme
NCR Manufacturing	Learning organisation
Nestle	Strategic alliances
Next Group	Core business concepts
Nissan	BPR/TQM

Name	Area of interest
Nixdorf	BPR
Nordstrom	Process redesign with IT
Northern Foods	BPR
P&O Ferries	Market positioning
Pearl Assurance	BPR
Pedigree Petfoods	Brand strategy
People Express	Job rotation/team management
Pepsi	Brand/positioning
Peugeot	Strategic alliances
Pilkington Optronics	BPR
Pizza Hut	Strategic alliances
Post Office Counters	BPR
Proctor & Gamble	Cultural change
Prudential Assurance	Downsizing
Quaker Oats	Flexible reward system
Rank Xerox	BPR/TQM BP simplification
Reuters	Customer, It-led, focus
Rolls-Royce Motor Cars	BPR
Rover Group Holdings	BPR
Rowntree	Reorganisation
Royal Dutch Shell	BPR
Saatchi & Saatchi	Market positioning/core business concepts
Sainsbury	Strategic alliances
SCO	BPR at software house for 'customer focus'
Sears Roebuck	Downsizing/ reorganisation
Semco	Radical BPR
Siemens Nixdorf Service	BPR
Smirnoff	Benchmarking
Smith's Crisps	BPR
SmithKline Beecham	Strategic change programme to 'stay ahead'
Sony Corporation	Innovative marketing strategies

Name	*Area of interest*
Southern Electric	Privatisation-led change programme/quality move
Spring Ram	Decentralisation in SBUs
Stella Artois	Brands
Sun Alliance	IT BPR (groupware)
Surrey Police Force	BPR
Swiss Bank Corporation	Culture change
Taco Bell	Empowerment and BPR
Texaco	IT-led BPR
Texas Instruments	BPR
The Contributions Agency	BPR
Toshiba	Strategic alliances
Toyota	Forging supplier relationships
TRW	BPR
TSB	Restructuring of management layers
Unilever	Product teams
United Airlines	Strategic alliances
United Grain Growers	IT-led BPR
Unitel	Outsourcing
US Steel	TQM
Virgin	'Reputation' as core business concept
Volkswagen	Reorganisation
Wal-Mart	BPR
Wella	BPR
Wessex Regional Health Authority	Outsourcing
Western Provincial Association	IT BPR programme
Westinghouse Corporation	TQ/BPR and process oriented
Whessoe	BPR
Wilkinson Sword	BPR
Zanussi	Strategy/market positioning
Zeneca	BPR

~ Appendix C ~
Comments from senior executives

"Not another management Bible; not another management cook-book. A short, positively stimulating read with which those who have 'been there' can easily identify, and full of extensive, practical advice for those who want to 'go there'."
David Rogers – Chief Executive, Amstrad plc

"This book successfully amalgamates all the business improvement approaches and ideas of the last two decades into a well written and concise guide. There are some radical suggestions for change which the authors have been brave enough to articulate, and these are offered as a challenge to progressive business leaders. The framework for Total Business Design (which incorporates a real understanding of resistance to change) is valuable."
Mike Alexander – Managing Director, British Gas plc, Public Gas Supply

"The book is fascinating and mould breaking. On first reading, I found it advised much which I had concluded from my own experience of actually making big corporate change. On second reading, there was much useful information which helped in expanding the core of Total Business Design. It is an excellent contribution to the theory and practice of change management."
Andrew Hoon – Chief Executive, Military Survey

"A thorough, well balanced and enjoyable read which pulls together many strands of business concepts to provide an approach to total review. I will encourage all my managers to read it."
Gordon Wareham – Chief Executive, Staffordshire Tableware

"This book will shake the management consulting industry."
Geoff Kitt, past President, Institute of Management Consultants

"This useful book provides a fresh and pragmatic approach to lasting business change. I liked its chatty style. Thought provoking!"
Philip Stapleton – European Strategic Planning Director, Hitachi

"I have read this book in great detail. I would like to re-assess our re-engineering programme in line with the thoughts of its authors."
Bryan McGinity – Managing Director, Triplex

"A comprehensive and readable summary of recent thinking on business transformation which places clear emphasis on the strategic framework, consistent communications and a 'learning' organisation."
David Garman – Managing Director, Allied Bakeries

"This book is the best example of a practical handbook aid that I have ever come across. Its style and layout make it a most friendly tool for the non-technician."
Sei James – Information Technology Director, TSB

"How refreshing to read a short handbook on current management ideas which enables busy senior executives to find their bearings when developing change strategies."
Gary Hawkes – Chief Executive, Gardner Merchant

"The book expertly points out the most practical way to learn hard lessons – through other managers' failures and successes. Bells ring loud and clear on every page."
Martin Shearman – Technical Director, NHS Pensions Agency

"Comprehensive coverage of issues in change management. Good insights (for example, Key Influencers) and excellent subsections (such as on Channels of Communication)."
Jeremy Watts – Managing Director, Armitage Shanks

"A stimulating read."
J A Doyle – Finance Director, Cherry Valley Farms Ltd

"This book challenges managers to rediscover sound principles of analysis (beware benchmarking), common sense (beware total quality) and firm leadership (beware empowerment). The authors canter through most management techniques and fads of recent years and warn of the dangers of management consultants."
Bryan Grey – Chief Executive, Baxi Partnership Ltd

"An entirely readable book with some very familiar situations and some less familiar. It appears to cover all the well known management techniques and some unusual ones. This book is the essential aide memoire for every manager's desk."
Peter Trevelyan – Chief Executive, Defence Accounts Agency

"Innovative and excellent."
Keith Mellor – IS Director, British Airports Authority

"An interesting book, well worth reading. Good lessons and well put across."
D A Stanley – Chief Executive, The Compensation Agency

"Rings all sorts of useful bells."
John Bullock – IS Services Director, British Nuclear Fuels plc

Index